WISDOM
FOR
TODAY'S ISSUES

A Topical Arrangement of the Proverbs

by

Stephen Voorwinde

Presbyterian and Reformed Publishing Co.
Phillipsburg, New Jersey 08865

ISBN: 0-87552-472-9

CONTENTS

PREFACE

To the modern Christian the Book of Proverbs may sometimes seem a bewildering array of wise and witty sayings compiled by the ancient Hebrews. Yet the truth of the matter is surely that this Book is replete with practical wisdom that is both timely and timeless. At times we find the format of Proverbs rather forbidding, and locating specific verses can be a frustrating experience. One of my aims in the present work has been to make this task easier for the average Bible reader.

In systematizing the Book of Proverbs I have sought to arrange in order the verses and passages dealing with its various themes and topics. In this attempt every verse in Proverbs has been included. Although Bible concordances were used, this work is not a concordance. I first went through Proverbs and listed every verse under one or more of the subject headings. The concepts of the resulting draft were then checked with the original Hebrew for every entry, and modifications were made. This was done in the interests of precision, correctness, and completeness.

As a young pastor in the gospel ministry I have found myself driven back to the Book of Proverbs time and again. Hence this work has grown out of a practical, pastoral need. It is my hope that through this effort the treasures of Proverbs will become more accessible and more appreciated. If this booklet helps believers to discern more accurately the Lord's revealed will for their daily lives, then my goal has been realized.

ABOMINATIONS

3:31,32

> Do not envy a man of violence,
> And do not choose any of his ways.
> [32] For the crooked man is an abomination to the
> LORD;
> But He is intimate with the upright.

6:16-19

> There are six things which the LORD hates,
> Yes, seven which are an abomination to Him:
> [17] Haughty eyes, a lying tongue,
> And hands that shed innocent blood,
> [18] A heart that devises wicked plans,
> Feet that run rapidly to evil,
> [19] A false witness who utters lies,
> And one who spreads strife among brothers.

8:7 (Wisdom speaking):

> "For my mouth will utter truth;
> And wickedness is an abomination to my
> lips."

11:1

> A false balance is an abomination to the LORD,
> But a just weight is His delight.

11:20

> The perverse in heart are an abomination to the
> LORD,
> But the blameless in their walk are His delight.

12:22

Lying lips are an abomination to the Lord.
But those who deal faithfully are His delight.

13:19

Desire realized is sweet to the soul,
But it is an abomination to fools to depart from
evil.

15:8,9

The sacrifice of the wicked is an abomination to the
Lord,
But the prayer of the upright is His delight.
[9]The way of the wicked is an abomination to the
Lord,
But He loves him who pursues righteousness.

15:26

Evil plans are an abomination to the Lord,
But pleasant words are pure.

16:5

Everyone who is proud in heart is an abomination
to the Lord;
Assuredly, he will not be unpunished.

16:12

It is an abomination for kings to commit
wickedness,
For a throne is established on righteousness.

17:15

He who justifies the wicked, and he who condemns
the righteous,
Both of them alike are an abomination to the Lord.

20:10

Differing weights and differing measures,
Both of them are abominable to the Lord.

2

20:23

>Differing weights are an abomination to the
>	LORD,
>And a false scale is not good.

21:27

>The sacrifice of the wicked in an abomination,
>How much more when he brings it with evil
>	intent!

24:9

>The devising of folly is sin,
>And the scoffer is an abomination to men.

26:24,25

>He who hates disguises it with his lips,
>But he lays up deceit in his heart.
>²⁵When he speaks graciously, do not believe him,
>For there are seven abominations in his heart.

28:9

>He who turns away his ear from listening to the law,
>Even his prayer is an abomination.

29:27

>An unjust man is abominable to the righteous,
>And he who is upright in the way is abominable to
>	the wicked.

ADULTERY

2:10,11,16-19

> For wisdom will enter your heart,
> And knowledge will be pleasant to your soul;
> [11] Discretion will guard you,
> Understanding will watch over you . . .
> [16] To deliver you from the strange woman,
> From the adulteress who flatters with her words;
> [17] That leaves the companion of her youth,
> And forgets the covenant of her God;
> [18] For her house sinks down to death,
> And her tracks lead to the dead;
> [19] None who go to her return again,
> Nor do they reach the paths of life.

5:1-23

> My son, give attention to my wisdom,
> Incline your ear to my understanding;
> [2] That you may observe discretion,
> And your lips may reserve knowledge.
> [3] For the lips of an adulteress drip honey,
> And smoother than oil is her speech;
> [4] But in the end she is bitter as wormwood,
> Sharp as a two-edged sword.
> [5] Her feet go down to death,
> Her steps lay hold of Sheol.
> [6] She does not ponder the path of life;
> Her ways are unstable, she does not know it.

4

[7]Now then, my sons, listen to me,
  And do not depart from the words of my mouth.
[8]Keep your way far from her,
  And do not go near the door of her house,
[9]Lest you give your vigor to others,
  And your years to the cruel one;
[10]Lest strangers be filled with your strength,
  And your hard-earned goods go to the house of an
    alien;
[11]And you groan at your latter end,
  When your flesh and your body are consumed;
[12]And you say, "How I have hated instruction!
  And my heart spurned reproof!
[13]"And I have not listened to the voice of my
    teachers,
  Nor inclined my ear to my instructors!
[14]"I was almost in utter ruin
  In the midst of the assembly and congregation."
[15]Drink water from your own cistern,
  And fresh water from your own well.
[16]Should your springs be dispersed abroad,
  Streams of water in the streets?
[17]Let them be yours alone,
  And not for strangers with you.
[18]Let your fountain be blessed,
  And rejoice in the wife of your youth.
[19]As a loving hind and a graceful doe,
  Let her breasts satisfy you at all times;
  Be exhilarated always with her love.
[20]For why should you, my son, be exhilarated with an
    adulteress,
  And embrace the bosom of a foreigner?
[21]For the ways of a man are before the eyes of the
    LORD,

5

And He watches all his paths.
²²His own iniquities will capture the wicked,
   And he will be held with the cords of his sin.
²³He will die for lack of instruction,
   And in the greatness of his folly he will go astray.

6:20-35

My son, observe the commandment of your father,
   And do not forsake the teaching of your mother;
²¹Bind them continually on your heart;
   Tie them around your neck.
²²When you walk about, they will guide you;
   When you sleep, they will watch over you;
   And when you awake, they will talk to you.
²³For the commandment is a lamp, and the teaching
      is light;
   And reproofs for discipline are the way of life,
²⁴To keep you from the evil woman,
   From the smooth tongue of the adulteress.
²⁵Do not desire her beauty in your heart,
   Nor let her catch you with her eyelids.
²⁶For on account of a harlot one is reduced to a loaf of
      bread,
   And an adulteress hunts for the precious life.
²⁷Can a man take fire in his bosom,
   And his clothes not be burned?
²⁸Or can a man walk on hot coals,
   And his feet not be scorched?
²⁹So is the one who goes in to his neighbor's wife;
   Whoever touches her will not go unpunished.
³⁰Men do not despise a thief if he steals
   To satisfy himself when he is hungry;
³¹But when he is found, he must repay sevenfold;
   He must give all the substance of his house.

³²The one who commits adultery with a woman is
        lacking sense;
  He who would destroy himself does it.
³³Wounds and disgrace he will find,
  And his reproach will not be blotted out.
³⁴For jealousy enrages a man,
  And he will not spare in the day of vengeance.
³⁵He will not accept any ransom,
  Nor will he be content though you give many gifts.

7:1-27

  My son, keep my words,
  And treasure my commandments within you.
²Keep my commandments and live,
  And my teaching as the apple of your eye.
³Bind them on your fingers;
  Write them on the tablet of your heart.
⁴Say to wisdom, "You are my sister,"
  And call understanding your intimate friend;
⁵That they may keep you from an adulteress,
  From the foreigner who flatters with her words.

⁶For at the window of my house
  I looked out through my lattice,
⁷And I saw among the naive,
  I discerned among the youths,
  A young man lacking sense,
⁸Passing through the street near her corner;
  And he takes the way to her house.
⁹In the twilight, in the evening,
  In the middle of the night and in the darkness.
¹⁰And behold, a woman comes to meet him,
  Dressed as a harlot and cunning of heart.
¹¹She is boisterous and rebellious;
  Her feet do not remain at home;

¹²She is now in the streets, now in the squares,
And lurks by every corner.
¹³So she seizes him and kisses him,
And with a brazen face she says to him:
¹⁴"I was due to offer peace offerings;
Today I have paid my vows.
¹⁵"Therefore I have come out to meet you,
To seek your presence earnestly, and I have found
you.
¹⁶"I have spread my couch with coverings,
With colored linens of Egypt.
¹⁷"I have sprinkled my bed
With myrrh, aloes and cinnamon.
¹⁸"Come, let us drink our fill of love until morning;
Let us delight ourselves with caresses.
¹⁹"For the man is not at home,
He has gone on a long journey;
²⁰He has taken a bag of money with him,
At full moon he will come home."
²¹With her many persuasions she entices him;
With her flattering lips she seduces him.
²²Suddenly he follows her,
As an ox goes to the slaughter,
Or as one in fetters to the discipline of a fool,
²³Until an arrow pierces through his liver;
As a bird hastens to the snare,
So he does not know that it will cost him his life.

²⁴Now therefore, my sons, listen to me,
And pay attention to the words of my mouth.
²⁵Do not let your heart turn aside to her ways,
Do not stray into her paths.
²⁶For many are the victims she has cast down,
And numerous are all her slain.
²⁷Her house is the way to Sheol,

Descending to the chambers of death.

9:13-18

The woman of folly is boisterous,
She is naive, and knows nothing.
¹⁴And she sits at the doorway of her house,
On a seat by the high places of the city,
¹⁵Calling to those who pass by,
Who are making their paths straight:
¹⁶"Whoever is naive, let him turn in here,"
And to him who lacks understanding she says,
¹⁷"Stolen water is sweet;
And bread eaten in secret is pleasant."
¹⁸But he does not know that the dead are there,
That her guests are in the depths of Sheol.

22:14

The mouth of an adulteress is a deep pit;
He who is cursed of the LORD will fall into it.

23:26-28

Give me your heart, my son,
And let your eyes delight in my ways.
²⁷For a harlot is a deep pit,
And an adulterous woman is a narrow well.
²⁸Surely she lurks as a robber,
And increases the faithless among men.

30:18-20

There are three things which are too wonderful for
me,
Four which I do not understand:
¹⁹The way of an eagle in the sky,
The way of a serpent on a rock,
The way of a ship in the middle of the sea,

And the way of a man with a maid.
[20]This is the way of an adulterous woman:
    She eats and wipes her mouth,
    And says, "I have done no wrong."

ALCOHOL

20:1

Wine is a mocker, strong drink a brawler,
And whoever is intoxicated by it is not wise.

21:17

He who loves pleasure will become a poor
    man;
He who loves wine and oil will not become rich.

23:19-21

Listen, my son, and be wise,
And direct your heart in the way.
[20]Do not be with heavy drinkers of wine,
Or with gluttonous eaters of meat;
[21]For the heavy drinker and the glutton will come to
    poverty,
And drowsiness will clothe a man with rags.

23:29-35

Who has woe? Who has sorrow?
Who has contentions? Who has complaining?
Who has wounds without cause?
Who has redness of eyes?
[30]Those who linger long over wine,
Those who go to taste mixed wine.
[31]Do not look on the wine when it is red,
When it sparkles in the cup,
When it goes down smoothly;

[32]At the last it bites like a serpent,
And stings like a viper.
[33]Your eyes will see strange things,
And your mind will utter perverse things.
[34]And you will be like one who lies down in the
middle of the sea,
Or like one who lies down on the top of a mast.
[35]"They struck me, but I did not become ill;
They beat me, but I did not know it.
When shall I awake?
I will seek another drink."

31:4-7

It is not for kings, O Lemuel,
It is not for kings to drink wine,
Or for rulers to desire strong drink.
[5]Lest they drink and forget what is decreed,
And pervert the rights of all the afflicted.
[6]Give strong drink to him who is perishing,
And wine to him whose life is bitter.
[7]Let him drink and forget his poverty,
And remember his trouble no more.

ANGER

6:34

> . . . jealousy enrages a man,
> And he will not spare in the day of vengeance.

14:17

> A quick-tempered man acts foolishly,
> And a man of evil devices is hated.

14:29

> He who is slow to anger has great understanding,
> But he who is quick-tempered exalts folly.

15:1

> A gentle answer turns away wrath,
> But a harsh word stirs up anger.

15:18

> A hot-tempered man stirs up strife,
> But the slow to anger pacifies contention.

16:14

> The wrath of a king is as messengers of death,
> But a wise man will appease it.

16:32

> He who is slow to anger is better than the mighty,
> And he who rules his spirit, than he who captures
> a city.

19:11

> A man's discretion makes him slow to anger,
> And it is his glory to overlook a transgression.

19:19

A man of great anger shall bear the penalty,
For if you rescue him, you will only have to do it
again.

21:14

A gift in secret subdues anger,
And a bribe in the bosom, strong wrath.

22:24,25

Do not associate with a man given to anger;
Or go with a hot-tempered man,
[25] Lest you learn his ways,
And find a snare for yourself.

24:17,18

Do not rejoice when your enemy falls,
And do not let your heart be glad when he
stumbles;
[18] Lest the LORD see it and be displeased,
And He turn away His anger from him.

27:4

Wrath is fierce and anger is a flood,
But who can stand before jealousy?

29:8

Scorners set a city aflame,
But wise men turn away anger.

29:22

An angry man stirs up strife,
And a hot-tempered man abounds in
transgression.

30:33

For the churning of milk produces butter,
And pressing the nose brings forth blood;
So the churning of anger produces strife.

BRIBERY

17:8

A bribe is a charm in the sight of its owner;
Wherever he turns, he prospers.

17:23

A wicked man receives a bribe from the bosom
To pervert the ways of justice.

21:14

A gift in secret subdues anger,
And a bribe in the bosom, strong wrath.

29:4

The king gives stability to the land by justice,
But a man who takes bribes overthrows it.

COUNSEL
(See also "Use of the Proverbs")

1:25,30-33 (Wisdom speaking):

> "And you neglected all my counsel,
> And did not want my reproof. . . .
> [30]"They would not accept my counsel,
> They spurned all my reproof.
> [31]"So they shall eat of the fruit of their own way,
> And be satiated with their own devices.
> [32]"For the waywardness of the naive shall kill them,
> And the complacency of fools shall destroy them.
> [33]"But he who listens to me shall live securely,
> And shall be at ease from the dread of evil."

8:14 (Wisdom speaking):

> "Counsel is mine and sound wisdom;
> I am understanding, power is mine."

12:15

> The way of a fool is right in his own eyes,
> But a wise man is he who listens to counsel.

13:10

> Through presumption comes nothing but strife,
> But with those who receive counsel is wisdom.

15:22

> Without consultation, plans are frustrated,
> But with many counselors they succeed.

19:20,21

Listen to counsel and accept discipline,
That you may be wise the rest of your days.
²¹Many are the plans in a man's heart,
But the counsel of the LORD, it will stand.

20:18

Prepare plans by consultation,
And make war by wise guidance.

21:30

There is no wisdom and no understanding
And no counsel against the LORD.

27:9

Oil and perfume make the heart glad,
So a man's counsel is sweet to his friend.

DECEIT

10:10

> He who winks the eye causes trouble.
> And a babbling fool will be thrown down.

12:5

> The thoughts of the righteous are just,
> But the counsels of the wicked are deceitful.

12:17

> He who speaks truth tells what is right,
> But a false witness, deceit.

12:20

> Deceit is in the heart of those who devise evil,
> But counselors of peace have joy.

14:8

> The wisdom of the prudent is to understand his
>   way,
> But the folly of fools is deceit.

16:30

> He who winks his eyes does so to devise perverse
>   things;
> He who compresses his lips brings evil to pass.

26:24-27

> He who hates disguises it with his lips,
> But he lays up deceit in his heart.

> [25]When he speaks graciously, do not believe him,

For there are seven abominations in his heart.
[26]Though his hatred covers itself with guile,
His wickedness will be revealed before the
assembly.
[27]He who digs a pit will fall into it,
And he who rolls a stone, it will come back on him

27:6

Faithful are the wounds of a friend,
But deceitful are the kisses of an enemy.

30:7,8

Two things I asked of Thee,
Do not refuse me before I die:
[8]Keep deception and lies far from me,
Give me neither poverty nor riches,
Feed me with the food that is my position.

DISCIPLINE

A. Discipline of Children

3:11,12

My son, do not reject the discipline of the LORD,
Or loathe His reproof,
¹²For whom the LORD loves He reproves,
Even as a father, the son in whom he delights.

13:1

A wise son accepts his father's discipline,
But a scoffer does not listen to rebuke.

13:24

He who spares his rod hates his son,
But he who loves him disciplines him diligently.

15:5

A fool rejects his father's discipline,
But he who regards reproof is prudent.

19:18

Discipline your son while there is hope,
And do not desire his death.

20:30

Stripes that wound scour away evil,
And strokes reach the innermost parts.

22:6

Train up a child in the way he should go,
Even when he is old he will not depart from it.

22:15

> Foolishness is bound up in the heart of a child;
> The rod of discipline will remove it far from him.

23:13,14

> Do not hold back discipline from the child,
> Although you beat him with the rod, he will not die.
> [14]You shall beat him with the rod,
> And deliver his soul from Sheol.

29:15

> The rod and reproof give wisdom,
> But a child who gets his own way brings shame to
>   his mother.

29:17

> Correct your son, and he will give you comfort;
> He will also delight your soul.

B. General

12:1

> Whoever loves discipline loves knowledge,
> But he who hates reproof is stupid.

13:18

> Poverty and shame will come to him who neglects
>   discipline,
> But he who regards reproof will be honored.

15:10

> Stern discipline is for him who forsakes the way;
> He who hates reproof will die.

15:31,32

> He whose ear listens to the life-giving reproof
> Will dwell among the wise.
> [32]He who neglects discipline despises himself,

But he who listens to reproof acquires understanding.

16:22

Understanding is a fountain of life to him who has it,
But the discipline of fools is folly.

17:10

A rebuke goes deeper into one who has understanding
Than a hundred blows into a fool.

19:20

Listen to counsel and accept discipline,
That you may be wise the rest of your days.

19:27

Cease listening, my son, to discipline,
And you will stray from the words of knowledge.

23:12

Apply your heart to discipline,
And your ears to the words of knowledge.

29:1

A man who hardens his neck after much reproof
Will suddenly be broken beyond remedy.

EDUCATION
(See also "Use of the Proverbs")

1:7-9

The fear of the LORD is the beginning of knowledge;
Fools despise wisdom and instruction.
[8] Hear, my son, your father's instruction,
And do not forsake your mother's teaching;
[9] Indeed, they are a graceful wreath to your head,
And ornaments about your neck.

2:4-6

If you seek her [wisdom] as silver,
And search for her as for hidden treasures;
[5] Then you will discern the fear of the LORD,
And discover the knowledge of God.
[6] For the LORD gives wisdom;
From His mouth come knowledge and
understanding.

4:10-13

Hear, my son, and accept my sayings,
And the years of your life will be many.
[11] I have directed you in the way of wisdom;
I have led you in upright paths.
[12] When you walk, your steps will not be impeded;
And if you run, you will not stumble.
[13] Take hold of instruction; do not let her go.
Guard her, for she is your life.

8:10-11 (Wisdom speaking):

> "Take my instruction, and not silver,
> And knowledge rather than choicest gold.
> [11] "For wisdom is better than jewels;
> And all desirable things can not compare with her."

8:33 (Wisdom speaking):

> "Heed instruction and be wise,
> And do not neglect it."

9:9

> Give instruction to a wise man, and he will be
> still wiser,
> Teach a righteous man, and he will increase his
> learning.

10:17

> He is on the path of life who heeds
> instruction,
> But he who forsakes reproof goes astray.

15:14

> The mind of the intelligent seeks knowledge,
> But the mouth of fools feeds on folly.

18:15

> The mind of the prudent acquires knowledge,
> And the ear of the wise seeks knowledge.

21:11

> When the scoffer is punished, the naive becomes
> wise;
> But when the wise is instructed, he receives
> knowledge.

23:12

> Apply your heart to discipline,
> And your ears to the words of knowledge.

23:23

> Buy truth, and do not sell it,
> Get wisdom and instruction and under-
>> standing.

27:17

> Iron sharpens iron,
> So one man sharpens another.

29:19

> A slave will not be instructed by words alone;
> For though he understands, there will be no
>> response.

EVIL

(See also "Abominations," "The Wicked")

1:10,15,16

My son, if sinners entice you,
Do not consent. . . .
[15] My son, do not walk in the way with them.
Keep your feet from their path,
[16] For their feet run to evil,
And they hasten to shed blood.

2:10-15

For wisdom will enter you heart,
And knowledge will be pleasant to your soul;
[11] Discretion will guard you,
Understanding will watch over you,
[12] To deliver you from the way of evil,
From the man who speaks perverse things;
[13] From those who leave the paths of uprightness,
To walk in the ways of darkness;
[14] Who delight in doing evil,
And rejoice in the perversity of evil;
[15] Whose paths are crooked,
And who are devious in their ways.

3:7

Do not be wise in your own eyes;
Fear the Lord and turn away from evil.

3:29,30

Do not devise harm against your neighbor,
While he lives in security beside you.

³⁰Do not contend with a man without cause,
If he has done you no harm.

4:14

Do not enter the path of the wicked,
And do not proceed in the way of evil men.

4:27

Do not turn to the right nor to the left;
Turn your foot from evil.

6:16-19

There are six things which the LORD hates,
Yes, seven which are an abomination to Him:
¹⁷Haughty eyes, a lying tongue,
And hands that shed innocent blood,
¹⁸A heart that devises wicked plans,
Feet that run rapidly to evil,
¹⁹A false witness who utters lies,
And one who spreads strife among brothers.

8:13 (Wisdom speaking):

"The fear of the LORD is to hate evil;
Pride and arrogance and the evil way,
And the perverted mouth, I hate."

11:19

He who is steadfast in righteousness will attain to life,
And he who pursues evil will bring about his own
    death.

11:21

Assuredly, the evil man will not go unpunished,
But the descendants of the righteous will be
    delivered.

11:27

He who diligently seeks good seeks favor,
But he who searches after evil, it will come to him.

12:13

An evil man is ensnared by the transgression of his
lips,
But the righteous will escape from trouble.

12:20

Deceit is in the heart of those who devise evil,
But counsellors of peace have joy.

13:19

Desire realized is sweet to the soul,
But it is an abomination to fools to depart from evil.

13:21

Adversity pursues sinners,
But the righteous will be rewarded with prosperity.

14:16,17

A wise man is cautious and turns away from
evil,
But a fool is arrogant and careless.
[17]A quick-tempered man acts foolishly,
And a man of evil devices is hated.

14:19

The evil will bow down before the good,
And the wicked at the gates of the righteous.

14:22

Will they not go astray who devise evil?
But kindness and truth will be to those who devise
good.

15:3

The eyes of the LORD are in every place,
Watching the evil and the good.

15:26

Evil plans are an abomination to the LORD,
But pleasant words are pure.

16:6

By lovingkindness and truth iniquity is atoned for.
And by the fear of the LORD one keeps away from
    evil.

16:17

The highway of the upright is to depart from evil:
He who watches his way preserves his life.

16:27

A worthless man digs up evil.
While his words are as a scorching fire.

16:30

He who winks his eyes does so to devise perverse
    things:
He who compresses his lips brings evil to pass.

17:11

A rebellious man seeks only evil.
So a cruel messenger will be sent against him.

17:13

He who returns evil for good.
Evil will not depart from his house.

17:20

He who has a crooked mind finds no good.
And he who is perverted in his language falls into evil.

19:23

The fear of the LORD leads to life.
So that one may sleep satisfied, untouched by evil.

20:8

A king who sits on the throne of justice
Disperses all evil with his eyes.

20:22

Do not say, "I will repay evil":
Wait for the LORD, and He will save you.

20:30

Stripes that wound scour away evil,
And strokes reach the innermost parts.

21:10

The soul of the wicked desires evil;
His neighbor finds no favor in his eyes.

22:3

The prudent sees the evil and hides himself,
But the naive go on, and are punished for it.

24:1,2

Do not be envious of evil men,
Nor desire to be with them;
[2]For their minds devise violence,
And their lips talk of trouble.

27:12

A prudent man sees evil and hides himself,
The naive proceed and pay the penalty.

28:5

Evil men do not understand justice,
But those who seek the Lord understand all things.

28:10

He who leads the upright astray in an evil way
Will himself fall into his own pit,
But the blameless will inherit good.

28:22

A man with an evil eye hastens after wealth,
And does not know that want will come upon him.

29:6

By transgression an evil man is ensnared,
But the righteous sings and rejoices.

31:12 (of the excellent wife)
She does him good and not evil
All the days of her life.

FEAR

1:33 (Wisdom speaking)

> ". . . he who listens to me shall live securely,
> And shall be at ease from the dread of evil."

3:24-26

> When you lie down, you will not be afraid;
> When you lie down, your sleep will be sweet.
> [25] Do not be afraid of sudden fear,
> Nor of the onslaught of the wicked when it comes;
> [26] For the LORD will be your confidence,
> And will keep your foot from being caught.

24:10

> If you are slack in the day of distress,
> Your strength is limited.

29:25

> The fear of man brings a snare,
> But he who trusts in the LORD will be exalted.

30:21-23

> Under three things the earth quakes,
> And under four, it cannot bear up:
> [22] Under a slave when he becomes a king,
> And a fool when he is satisfied with food,
> [23] Under an unloved woman when she gets a
> husband,
> And a maidservant when she supplants her
> mistress.

THE FEAR OF THE LORD

1:7

> The fear of the LORD is the beginning of knowledge;
> Fools despise wisdom and instruction.

1:28,29 (Wisdom speaking)

> "Then they will call on me, but I will not answer;
> They will seek me diligently, but they shall not find
>   me,
> [29]Because they hated knowledge,
> And did not choose the fear of the LORD."

2:1-5

> My son, if you will receive my sayings,
> And treasure my commandments within
>   you,
> [2]Make your ear attentive to wisdom,
> Incline your heart to understanding;
> [3]For if you cry for discernment,
> Lift your voice for understanding;
> [4]If you seek her as silver,
> And search for her as for hidden treasures;
> [5]Then you will discern the fear of the LORD,
> And discover the knowledge of God.

3:7,8

> Do not be wise in your own eyes;
> Fear the LORD and turn away from evil.
> [8]It will be healing to your body,
> And refreshment to your bones.

8:13a

> The fear of the LORD is to hate evil.

9:10

The fear of the LORD is the beginning of wisdom,
And the knowledge of the Holy One is
understanding.

10:27

The fear of the LORD prolongs life,
But the years of the wicked will be shortened.

13:13

The one who despises the word will be in debt to it,
But the one who fears the commandment will be
rewarded.

14:2

He who walks in his uprightness fears the LORD,
But he who is crooked in his ways despises Him.

14:26,27

In the fear of the LORD there is strong confidence,
And his children will have refuge.
[27] The fear of the LORD is a fountain of life,
That one may avoid the snares of death.

15:16

Better is a little with the fear of the LORD,
Than great treasure and turmoil with it.

15:33

The fear of the LORD is the instruction for wisdom,
And before honor comes humility.

16:6

By lovingkindness and truth iniquity is atoned for,
And by the fear of the LORD one keeps away from
evil.

19:23

The fear of the LORD leads to life,
So that one may sleep satisfied, untouched by evil.

22:4

> The reward of humility and the fear of the LORD
> Are riches, honor and life

23:17,18

> Do not let your heart envy sinners,
> But live in the fear of the LORD always.
> ¹⁸Surely there is a future,
> And your hope will not be cut off.

24:21,22

> My son, fear the LORD and the king;
> Do not associate with those who are given to
> change;
> ²²For their calamity will rise suddenly,
> And who knows the ruin that comes from both of
> them?

28:14

> How blessed is the man who fears always,
> But he who hardens his heart will fall into calamity.

29:25

> The fear of man brings a snare
> But he who trusts in the LORD will be exalted.

31:30

> Charm is deceitful and beauty is vain,
> But a woman who fears the LORD, she shall be
> praised.

FOOD

12:11

    He who tills his land will have plenty of bread,
    But he who pursues vain things lacks sense.

20:13

    Do not love sleep, lest you become poor;
    Open your eyes, and you will be satisfied with food.

20:17

    Bread obtained by falsehood is sweet to a man,
    But afterward his mouth will be filled with gravel.

22:9

    He who is generous will be blessed,
    For he gives some of his food to the poor.

23:1-3

    When you sit down to dine with a ruler,
    Consider carefully what is before you;
[2]And put a knife to your throat,
    If you are a man of great appetite.
[3]Do not desire his delicacies,
    For it is deceptive food.

23:6-8

    Do not eat the bread of a selfish man,
    Or desire his delicacies;
[7]For as he thinks within himself, so he is.
    He says to you, "Eat and drink!"
    But his heart is not with you.
[8]You will vomit up the morsel you have eaten,
    And waste your compliments.

23:19-21

Listen, my son, and be wise,
And direct your heart in the way.
²⁰Do not be with heavy drinkers of wine,
Or with gluttonous eaters of meat;
²¹For the heavy drinker and the glutton
will come to poverty,
And drowsiness will clothe a man with rags.

24:13,14

My son, eat honey, for it is good,
Yes, the honey from the comb is sweet to your
taste;
¹⁴Know that wisdom is thus for your soul;
If you find it, then there will be a future,
And your hope will not be cut off.

25:16

Have you found honey? Eat only what you need,
Lest you have it in excess and vomit it.

25:21,22

If your enemy is hungry, give him food to eat;
And if he is thirsty, give him water to drink;
²²For you will heap burning coals on his head,
And the LORD will reward you.

27:7

A sated man loathes honey,
But to a famished man any bitter thing is sweet.

27:23-27

Know well the condition of your flocks,
And pay attention to your herds;
²⁴For riches are not forever,
Nor does a crown endure to all generations.
²⁵When the grass disappears, the new growth is seen,

And the herbs of the mountains are gathered in,
²⁶The lambs will be for your clothing,
And the goats will bring the price of a field,
²⁷And there will be goats' milk enough for your food,
For the food of your household,
And sustenance for your maidens.

28:19

He who tills his land will have plenty of food,
But he who follows empty pursuits will have poverty
in plenty.

30:7-9

Two things I asked of Thee,
Do not refuse me before I die:
⁸Keep deception and lies far from me,
Give me neither poverty nor riches;
Feed me with the food that is my portion,
⁹Lest I be full and deny Thee and say, "Who is the
LORD?"
Or lest I be in want and steal,
And profane the name of my God.

31:14,15 (of the excellent wife)

She is like the merchant ships;
She brings her food from afar.
¹⁵She rises also while it is still night,
And gives food to her household,
And portions to her maidens.

THE FOOL

A. General

1:7

>The fear of the LORD is the beginning of knowledge;
>Fools despise wisdom and instruction.

1:32 (Wisdom speaking)

>"For the waywardness of the naive shall kill them,
>And the complacency of fools shall destroy them."

8:5,6 (Wisdom speaking)

>"O naive ones, discern prudence;
>And, O fools, discern wisdom.
>⁶"Listen, for I shall speak noble things;
>And the opening of my lips will produce right
>   things."

10:10

>He who winks the eye causes trouble,
>And a babbling fool will be thrown down.

10:18

>He who conceals hatred has lying lips,
>And he who spreads slander is a fool.

11:29

>He who troubles his own house will inherit wind,
>And the foolish will be servant to the wisehearted.

13:19

>Desire realized is sweet to the soul,

But it is an abomination to fools to depart from evil.

16:22

Understanding is a fountain of life to him who has
it,
But the discipline of fools is folly.

17:7

Excellent speech is not fitting for a fool;
Much less are lying lips to a prince.

17:12

Let a man meet a bear robbed of her cubs,
Rather than a fool in his folly.

17:16

Why is there a price in the hand of a fool to buy
wisdom,
When he has no sense?

17:21

He who begets a fool does so to his sorrow,
And the father of a fool has no joy.

17:25

A foolish son is a grief to his father,
And bitterness to her who bore him.

17:28

Even a fool, when he keeps silent, is considered
wise;
When he closes his lips, he is counted prudent.

18:2

A fool does not delight in understanding,
But only in revealing his own mind.

18:6,7

A fool's lips bring strife,
And his mouth calls for blows.

⁷A fool's mouth is his ruin,
And his lips are the snare of his soul.

19:1

Better is a poor man who walks in his integrity
Than he who is perverse in speech and is a
fool.

19:10

Luxury is not fitting for a fool;
Much less for a slave to rule over princes.

19:13

A foolish son is destruction to his father,
And the contentions of a wife are a constant
dripping.

19:29

Judgments are prepared for scoffers,
And blows for the backs of fools.

20:3

Keeping away from strife is an honor for a
man,
But any fool will quarrel.

23:9

Do not speak in the hearing of a fool,
For he will despise the wisdom of your words.

24:7

Wisdom is too high for a fool,
He does not open his mouth in the gate.

26:1-12

Like snow in summer and like rain in harvest,
So honor is not fitting for a fool.
²Like a sparrow in its flitting, like a swallow
in its flying,
So a curse without cause does not alight.

³A whip is for the horse, a bridle for the donkey,
  And a rod for the back of fools.
⁴Do not answer a fool according to his folly,
  Lest you also be like him.
⁵Answer a fool as his folly deserves,
  Lest he be wise in his own eyes.
⁶He cuts off his own feet, and drinks violence
  Who sends a message by the hand of a fool.
⁷Like the legs which hang down from the
      lame,
  So is a proverb in the mouth of fools.
⁸Like one who binds a stone in a sling,
  So is he who gives honor to a fool.
⁹Like a thorn which falls into the hand of a drunkard,
  So is a proverb in the mouth of fools.
¹⁰Like an archer who wounds everyone,
  So is he who hires a fool or who hires those who
      pass by.
¹¹Like a dog that returns to its vomit
  Is a fool who repeats his folly.
¹²Do you see a man wise in his own eyes?
  There is more hope for a fool than for him.

27:3

A stone is heavy and the sand weighty,
But the provocation of a fool is heavier than both of
    them.

27:22

Though you pound a fool in a mortar with a pestle
    along with crushed grain,
Yet his folly will not depart from him.

29:20

Do you see a man who is hasty in his words?
There is more hope for a fool than for him.

B. The Fool versus the Prudent, the Righteous and the Wise

3:35

> The wise will inherit honor,
> But fools display dishonor.

10:1

> A wise son makes a father glad,
> But a foolish son is a grief to his mother.

10:8

> The wise of heart will receive commands,
> But a babbling fool will be thrown down.

10:14

> Wise men store up knowledge,
> But with the mouth of the foolish, ruin is at
>   hand.

10:21

> The lips of the righteous feed many,
> But fools die for lack of understanding.

10:23

> Doing wickedness is like sport to a fool;
> And so is wisdom to a man of understanding.

12:15,16

> The way of a fool is right in his own eyes,
> But a wise man is he who listens to counsel.
> [16]A fool's vexation is known at once,
> But a prudent man conceals dishonor.

12:23

> A prudent man conceals knowledge,
> But the heart of fools proclaims folly.

13:16

> Every prudent man acts with knowledge,
> But a fool displays folly.

13:20

He who walks with wise men will be wise,
But the companion of fools will suffer harm.

14:3

In the mouth of the foolish is a rod for his back,
But the lips of the wise will preserve them.

14:7-9

Leave the presence of a fool,
Or you will not discern words of knowledge.
[8]The wisdom of the prudent is to understand his
way,
But the folly of fools is deceit.
[9]Fools mock at sin,
But among the upright there is good will.

14:16

A wise man is cautious and turns away from evil,
But a fool is arrogant and careless.

14:24

The crown of the wise is their riches,
But the folly of fools is foolishness.

14:33

Wisdom rests in the heart of one who has
understanding,
But in the bosom of fools it is made known.

15:2

The tongue of the wise makes knowledge
acceptable,
But the mouth of fools spouts folly.

15:5

A fool rejects his father's discipline,
But he who regards reproof is prudent.

15:7

The lips of the wise spread knowledge,
But the hearts of fools are not so.

15:14

The mind of the intelligent seeks knowledge,
But the mouth of fools feeds on folly.

15:20

A wise son makes a father glad,
But a foolish man despises his mother.

17:10

A rebuke goes deeper into one who has
        understanding
Than a hundred blows into a fool.

17:24

Wisdom is in the presence of the one who has
        understanding,
But the eyes of a fool are on the ends of the earth.

21:20

There is precious treasure and oil in the dwelling of
        the wise,
But a foolish man swallows it up.

28:26

He who trusts in his own heart is a fool,
But he who walks wisely will be delivered.

29:9

When a wise man has a controversy with a foolish
        man,
The foolish man either rages or laughs, and
        there is no rest.

29:11

A fool always loses his temper,
But a wise man holds it back.

FRIENDS AND NEIGHBORS*

3:27-29

Do not withhold good from those to whom it is due,
When it is in your power to do it.
²⁸Do not say to your neighbor, "Go, and come back,
And tomorrow I will give it,"
When you have it with you.
²⁹Do not devise harm against your neighbor,
While he lives in security beside you.

6:1-3

My son, if you have become surety for your
neighbor,
Have given a pledge for a stranger,
²If you have been snared with the words of your
mouth,
Have been caught with the words of your mouth,
³Do this then, my son, and deliver yourself:
Since you have come into the hand of your neighbor,
Go, humble yourself, and importune your neighbor.

6:27-29

Can a man take fire in his bosom,
And his clothes not be burned?
²⁸Or can a man walk on hot coals,
And his feet not be scorched?
²⁹So is the one who goes in to his neighbor's wife:
Whoever touches her will not go unpunished.

_____

*These two English words are used to translate a single Hebrew word
in the original. Where a different Hebrew word has been used in the
original an alternate English meaning has been given in brackets (see
18:24; 27:6,10).

11:9

> With his mouth the godless man destroys his
>> neighbor.
> But through knowledge the righteous will be
>> delivered.

11:12

> He who despises his neighbor lacks sense.
> But a man of understanding keeps silent.

12:26

> The righteous is a guide to his
>> neighbor.
> But the way of the wicked leads them astray.

14:20,21

> The poor is hated even by his neighbor,
> But those who love the rich are many.
> [21] He who despises his neighbor sins,
> But happy is he who is gracious to the poor.

16:29

> A man of violence entices his neighbor,
> And leads him in a way that is not good.

17:17,18

> A friend loves at all times,
> And a brother is born for adversity.
> [18] A man lacking in sense pledges,
> And becomes surety in the presence of his
>> neighbor.

18:17

> The first to plead his case seems just,
> Until another comes and examines him.

18:24

> A man of many friends comes to ruin,

But there is a friend [lover] who sticks closer than a
　　brother.

19:4

Wealth adds many friends,
But a poor man is separated from his
　　friend.

19:6

Many will entreat the favor of a generous man,
And every man is a friend to him who gives gifts.

21:10

The soul of the wicked desires evil;
His neighbor finds no favor in his eyes.

22:11

He who loves purity of heart
And whose speech is gracious, the king is his friend.

24:28,29

Do not be a witness against your neighbor without
　　cause,
And do not deceive with your lips.
[29]Do not say, "Thus I shall do to him as he has done
　　to me;
I will render to the man according to his work."

25:8-10

Do not go out hastily to argue your case;
Otherwise, what will you do in the end,
When your neighbor puts you to shame?
[9]Argue your case with your neighbor,
And do not reveal the secret of another,
[10]Lest he who hears it reproach you,
And the evil report about you not pass away.

25:17,18

Let your foot rarely be in your neighbor's house,

Lest he become weary of you and hate you.
[18]Like a club and a sword and a sharp arrow
Is a man who bears false witness against his
neighbor.

26:18,19

Like a madman who throws
Firebrands, arrows and death,
[19]So is the man who deceives his neighbor,
And says, "Was I not joking?"

27:6

Faithful are the wounds of a friend [lover],
But deceitful are the kisses of an enemy.

27:9,10

Oil and perfume make the heart glad,
So a man's counsel is sweet to his friend.
[10]Do not forsake your own friend or your father's
friend,
And do not go to your brother's house in the day of
your calamity;
Better is a neighbor who is near (he who dwells
near) than a brother far away.

27:14

He who blesses his friend with a loud voice early
in the morning,
It will be reckoned a curse to him.

27:17

Iron sharpens iron,
So one man sharpens another.

29:5

A man who flatters his neighbor
Is spreading a net for his steps.

THE FUTURE

10:28

The hope of the righteous is gladness,
But the expectation of the wicked perishes.

11:23

The desire of the righteous is only good,
But the expectation of the wicked is wrath.

13:12

Hope deferred makes the heart sick,
But desire fulfilled is a tree of life.

21:31

The horse is prepared for the day of battle,
But victory belongs to the LORD.

23:17,18

Do not let your heart envy sinners,
But live in the fear of the LORD always.
[18]Surely there is a future,
And your hope will not be cut off.

24:13,14

My son, eat honey, for it is good,
Yes, the honey from the comb is sweet to your
        taste;
[14]Know that wisdom is thus for your soul;
If you find it, then there will be a future,
And your hope will not be cut off.

24:19,20

Do not fret yourself because of evildoers,
Or be envious of the wicked;
[20] For there will be no future for the evil man;
The lamp of the wicked will be put out.

27:1

Do not boast about tomorrow,
For you do not know what a day may bring forth.

31:25 (Of the excellent wife)

Strength and dignity are her clothing,
And she smiles at the future.

GIVING

3:27,28

Do not withhold good from those to whom it is
due,
When it is in your power to do it.
²⁸Do not say to your neighbor, "Go, and come back,
And tomorrow I will give it,"
When you have it with you.

11:24,25

There is one who scatters, yet increases all the
more,
And there is one who withholds what is justly due,
but it results only in want.
²⁵The generous man will be prosperous,
And he who waters will himself be watered.

14:31

He who oppresses the poor reproaches his Maker,
But he who is gracious to the needy honors Him.

18:16

A man's gift makes room for him,
And brings him before great men.

19:6

Many will entreat the favor of a generous man,
And every man is a friend to him who gives gifts.

19:17

He who is gracious to a poor man lends to the
LORD,
And He will repay him for his good deed.

21:25,26

> The desire of the sluggard puts him to death,
> For his hands refuse to work;
> [26] All day long he is craving.
> While the righteous gives and does not hold back.

22:9

> He who is generous will be blessed,
> For he gives some of his food to the poor.

28:27

> He who gives to the poor will never want,
> But he who shuts his eyes will have many curses.

GREED

11:6

The righteousness of the upright will diliver them,
But the treacherous will be caught by their own
greed

11:26

He who withholds grain, the people will curse him,
But blessing will be on the head of him who sells it.

27:20

Sheol and Abaddon are never satisfied
Nor are the eyes of man ever satisfied.

30:15,16

The leech has two daughters,
"Give," "Give."
There are three things that will not be satisfied,
Four that will not say, "Enough":
[16]Sheol, and the barren womb,
Earth that is never satisfied with water,
And fire that never says, "Enough."

GUIDANCE

3:5,6

Trust in the LORD with all your heart,
And do not lean on your own understanding.
[6]In all your ways acknowledge Him,
And He will make your paths straight.

11:3

The integrity of the upright will guide them,
But the falseness of the treacherous will destroy
them.

11:14

Where there is no guidance, the people fall,
But in abundance of counselors there is victory.

14:12 and 16:25

There is a way which seems right to a man,
But its end is the way of death.

16:33

The lot is cast into the lap,
But its every decision is from the LORD.

20:18

Prepare plans by consultation,
And make war by wise guidance.

20:24

Man's steps are ordained by the LORD,
How then can man understand his way?

24:5,6

A wise man is strong,
And a man of knowledge increases power.
[6]For by wise guidance you will wage war,
And in abundance of counselors there is victory.

HEART

2:2

    Make your ear attentive to wisdom,
    Incline your heart to understanding.

3:1

    My son, do not forget my teaching,
    But let your heart keep my commandments.

3:3

    Do not let kindness and truth leave you;
    Bind them around your neck,
    Write them on the tablet of your heart.

3:5

    Trust in the LORD with all your heart,
    And do not lean on your own understanding.

4:20-23

    My son, give attention to my words;
    Incline your ear to my sayings.
[21]Do not let them depart from your sight;
    Keep them in the midst of your heart.
[22]For they are life to those who find them,
    And health to all their whole body.
[23]Watch over your heart with all diligence,
    For from it flow the springs of life.

6:16-19

    There are six things which the LORD hates,
    Yes, seven which are an abomination to Him:
[17]Haughty eyes, a lying tongue,
    And hands that shed innocent blood,

^{18}A heart that devises wicked plans,
Feet that run rapidly to evil,
^{19}A false witness who utters lies,
And one who spreads strife among brothers.

6:20,21

My son, observe the commandment of your father,
And do not forsake the teaching of your mother;
^{21}Bind them continually on your heart;
Tie them around your neck.

7:2,3

Keep my commandments and live,
And my teaching as the apple of your eye.
^{3}Bind them on your fingers;
Write them on the tablet of your heart.

10:20

The tongue of the righteous is as choice silver,
The heart of the wicked is worth little.

11:20

The perverse in heart are an abomination to the
LORD,
But the blameless in their walk are His delight.

11:29

He who troubles his own house will inherit wind,
And the foolish will be servant to the wisehearted.

12:20

Deceit is in the heart of those who devise evil,
But counselors of peace have joy.

12:23

A prudent man conceals knowledge,
But the heart of fools proclaims folly.

12:25

Anxiety in the heart of a man weighs it down,
But a good word makes it glad.

13:12

Hope deferred makes the heart sick,
But desire fulfilled is a tree of life.

14:10

The heart knows its own bitterness,
And a stranger does not share its joy.

14:13,14

Even in laughter the heart may be in pain,
And the end of joy may be grief.
[14]The backslider in heart will have his fill of his own
   ways,
But a good man will be satisfied with his.

14:30

A tranquil heart is life to the body,
But passion is rottenness to the bones.

14:33

Wisdom rests in the heart of one who has
   understanding,
But in the bosom of fools it is made known.

15:7

The lips of the wise spread knowledge,
But the hearts of fools are not so.

15:11

Sheol and Abaddon lie open before the LORD,
How much more the hearts of men!

15:13

A joyful heart makes a cheerful face,
But when the heart is sad, the spirit is broken.

15:15

>All the days of the afflicted are bad,
>But a cheerful heart has a continual feast.

15:28

>The heart of the righteous ponders how to answer,
>But the mouth of the wicked pours out evil things.

15:30

>Bright eyes gladden the heart;
>Good news puts fat on the bones.

16:1,2

>The plans of the heart belong to man,
>But the answer of the tongue is from the LORD.
>²All the ways of a man are clean in his own sight,
>But the LORD weighs the motives.

16:5

>Everyone who is proud in heart is an abomination
>   to the LORD;
>Assuredly, he will not be unpunished.

16:21

>The wise in heart will be called discerning,
>And sweetness of speech increases persuasiveness.

16:23

>The heart of the wise teaches his mouth,
>And adds persuasiveness to his lips.

17:3

>The refining pot is for silver and the furnace for
>   gold,
>But the LORD tests hearts.

17:22

>A joyful heart is good medicine,
>But a broken spirit dries up the bones

18:12

Before destruction the heart of man is haughty.
But humility goes before honor.

18:14

The spirit of a man can endure his sickness.
But a broken spirit who can bear?

19:3

The foolishness of man subverts his way.
And his heart rages against the LORD.

19:21

Many are the plans in a man's heart.
But the counsel of the LORD. it will stand.

20:5

A plan in the heart of a man is like deep water.
But a man of understanding draws it out.

20:9

Who can say. "I have cleansed my heart.
I am pure from my sin"?

21:1,2

The king's heart is like channels of water in the
        hand of the LORD:
He turns it wherever He wishes.
²Every man's way is right in his own eyes.
But the LORD weighs the hearts.

21:4

Haughty eyes and a proud heart.
The lamp of the wicked. is sin.

22:11

He who loves purity of heart
And whose speech is gracious. the king is his friend.

22:15

Foolishness is bound up in the heart of a child;
The rod of discipline will remove it far from him.

23:12

Apply your heart to discipline,
And your ears to words of knowledge.

23:15,16

My son, if your heart is wise,
My own heart also will be glad;
[16]And my inmost being will rejoice,
When your lips speak what is right.

23:17

Do not let your heart envy sinners,
But live in the fear of the LORD always.

23:26

Give me your heart, my son,
And let your eyes delight in my ways.

24:17

Do not rejoice when your enemy falls,
And do not let your heart be glad when he
stumbles.

25:3

As the heavens for height and the earth for depth,
So the heart of kings is unsearchable.

25:20

Like one who takes off a garment on a cold day, or
like vinegar on soda,
Is he who sings songs to a troubled heart.

26:23-25

Like an earthen vessel overlaid with silver dross
Are burning lips and a wicked heart.

²⁴He who hates disguises it with his lips,
But he lays up deceit in his heart.
²⁵When he speaks graciously, do not believe him,
For there are seven abominations in his heart.

27:9

Oil and perfume make the heart glad,
So a man's counsel is sweet to his friend.

27:11

Be wise, my son, and make my heart glad,
That I may reply to him who reproaches me.

27:19

As in water face reflects face,
So the heart of man reflects man.

28:14

How blessed is the man who fears always,
But he who hardens his heart will fall into calamity.

28:26

He who trusts in his own heart is a fool,
But he who walks wisely, will be delivered.

31:10,11

An excellent wife, who can find?
For her worth is far above jewels.
¹¹The heart of her husband trusts in her,
And he will have no lack of gain.

THE HOME

(See also "Parents," "Woman")

3:33

> The curse of the LORD is on the house of the
> wicked,
> But He blesses the dwelling of the righteous.

11:29

> He who troubles his own house will inherit wind,
> And the foolish will be servant to the wisehearted.

12:7

> The wicked are overthrown and are no more,
> But the house of the righteous will stand.

14:1

> The wise woman builds her house,
> But the foolish tears it down with her own hands.

14:11

> The house of the wicked will be destroyed,
> But the tent of the upright will flourish.

15:6

> Much wealth is in the house of the righteous,
> But trouble is in the income of the wicked.

15:17

> Better is a dish of vegetables where love is,
> Than a fattened ox and hatred with it.

15:25

> The LORD will tear down the house of the proud,
> But He will establish the boundary of the widow.

15:27

He who profits illicitly troubles his own house,
But he who hates bribes will live.

17:1,2

Better is a dry morsel and quietness with it
Than a house full of feasting with strife.
²A servant who acts wisely will rule over a son who
acts shamefully,
And will share in the inheritance among brothers.

17:17

A friend loves at all times,
And a brother is born for adversity.

18:19

A brother offended is harder to be won than a
strong city,
And contentions are like the bars of a castle.

19:13,14

A foolish son is destruction to his father,
And the contentions of a wife are a constant
dripping.
¹⁴House and wealth are an inheritance from fathers,
But a prudent wife is from the LORD.

21:9 and 25:24

It is better to live in a corner of a roof,
Than in a house shared with a contentious woman.

21:12

The righteous one considers the house of the
wicked,
Turning the wicked to ruin.

24:3,4

By wisdom a house is built,
And by understanding it is established;

[4]And by knowledge the rooms are filled
With all precious and pleasant riches.

27:8

Like a bird that wanders from her nest,
So is a man who wanders from his home.

29:21

He who pampers his slave from childhood
Will in the end find him to be a son.

HONESTY

11:1

> A false balance is an abomination to the LORD,
> But a just weight is His delight.

16:11

> A just balance and scales belong to the LORD;
> All the weights of the bag are His concern.

20:6,7

> Many a man proclaims his own loyalty,
> But who can find a trustworthy man?
> ⁷A righteous man who walks in his integrity—
> How blessed are his sons after him.

20:10

> Differing weights and differing measures,
> Both of them are abominable to the LORD.

20:17

> Bread obtained by falsehood is sweet to a man,
> But afterward his mouth will be filled with gravel.

20:23

> Differing weights are an abomination to the LORD,
> And a false scale is not good.

25:19

> Like a bad tooth and an unsteady foot
> Is confidence in a faithless man in time of trouble.

HONOR

3:16 (Of Wisdom)
> Long life is in her right hand;
> In her left hand are riches and honor.

3:35
> The wise will inherit honor,
> But fools display dishonor.

8:18 (Wisdom speaking)
> "Riches and honor are with me,
> Enduring wealth and righteousness."

10:7
> The memory of the righteous is blessed,
> But the name of the wicked will rot.

11:16
> A gracious woman attains honor,
> And violent men attain riches.

12:8,9
> A man will be praised according to his insight,
> But one of perverse mind will be despised.
> [9]Better is he who is lightly esteemed and has a
>   servant,
> Than he who honors himself and lacks bread.

12:16
> A fool's vexation is known at once,
> But a prudent man conceals dishonor.

15:33

The fear of the LORD is the instruction for wisdom,
And before honor comes humility.

18:3

When a wicked man comes, contempt also comes,
And with dishonor comes reproach.

18:12

Before destruction the heart of man is haughty,
But humility goes before honor.

20:3

Keeping away from strife is an honor for a man,
But any fool will quarrel.

20:29

The glory of young men is their strength,
And the honor of old men is their gray hair.

21:21

He who pursues righteousness and loyalty
Finds life, righteousness and honor.

22:1

A good name is to be more desired than great
riches,
Favor is better than silver and gold.

22:4

The reward of humility and the fear of the LORD
Are riches, honor and life.

25:27

It is not good to eat much honey,
Nor is it glory to search out one's own glory.

26:1

Like snow in summer and like rain in harvest,
So honor is not fitting for a fool.

26:8

> Like one who binds a stone in a sling,
> So is he who gives honor to a fool.

27:2

> Let another praise you, and not your own mouth;
> A stranger, and not your own lips.

27:21

> The crucible is for silver and the furnace for gold,
> And a man is tested by the praise accorded him.

29:23

> A man's pride will bring him low,
> But a humble spirit will obtain honor.

HUNGER

10:3

The Lord will not allow the righteous to hunger,
But He will thrust aside the craving of the wicked.

13:23

Abundant food is in the fallow ground of the poor,
But it is swept away by injustice.

13:25

The righteous has enough to satisfy his appetite,
But the stomach of the wicked is in want.

19:15

Laziness casts into a deep sleep,
And an idle man will suffer hunger.

25:21

If your enemy is hungry, give him food to eat;
And if he is thirsty, give him water to drink.

27:7

A sated man loathes honey,
But to a famished man any bitter thing is sweet.

JUSTICE

(See also "Use of the Proverbs")

8:15 (Wisdom speaking)
"By me kings reign,
And rulers decree justice."

18:5

To show partiality to the wicked is not good,
Nor to thrust aside the righteous in judgment.

18:17,18

The first to plead his case seems just,
Until another comes and examines him.
[18]The lot puts an end to contentions,
And decides between the mighty.

21:3

To do righteousness and justice
Is desired by the LORD rather than sacrifice.

21:15

The execution of justice is joy for the righteous,
But is terror to the workers of iniquity.

22:22,23

Do not rob the poor because he is poor,
Or crush the afflicted at the gate;
[23]For the LORD will plead their case,
And take the life of those who rob them.

22:28

Do not move the ancient boundary
Which your fathers have set.

23:10,11

Do not move the ancient boundary,
Or go into the fields of the fatherless;
[11]For their Redeemer is strong;
He will plead their case against you.

24:11,12

Deliver those who are being taken away to death,
And those who are staggering to slaughter, O hold
them back.
[12]If you say, "See, we did not know this,"
Does He not consider it who weighs the hearts?
And does He not know it who keeps your soul?
And will He not render to man according to his
work?

24:23-26

These also are sayings of the wise.
To show partiality in judgment is not good.
[24]He who says to the wicked, "You are righteous,"
Peoples will curse him, nations will abhor him;
[25]But to those who rebuke the wicked will be delight,
And a good blessing will come upon them.
[26]He kisses the lips
Who gives a right answer.

28:5

Evil men do not understand justice,
But those who seek the LORD understand all things.

28:21

To show partiality is not good,
Because for a piece of bread a man will transgress.

29:26,27

Many seek the ruler's favor,
But justice for man comes from the LORD.

[27] An unjust man is abominable to the righteous,
   And he who is upright in the way is abominable to
      the wicked.

31:8,9 (To King Lemuel)
   Open your mouth for the dumb,
   For the rights of all the unfortunate.
   [9] Open your mouth, judge righteously,
   And defend the rights of the afflicted and needy.

KINDNESS

3:3,4

Do not let kindness* and truth leave you;
Bind them around your neck,
Write them on the tablet of your heart.
⁴So you will find favor and good repute
In the sight of God and man.

11:17

The merciful* man does himself good,
But the cruel man does himself harm.

14:22

Will they not go astray who devise evil?
But kindness* and truth will be to those who devise
good.

16:6

By lovingkindness* and truth iniquity is atoned for,
And by the fear of the LORD one keeps away from
evil.

19:22

What is desirable in a man is his kindness,*
And it is better to be a poor man than a liar.

20:6

Many a man proclaims his own loyalty,*
But who can find a trustworthy man?

20:28

Loyalty* and truth preserve the king,
And he upholds his throne by righteousness.*

21:21
> He who pursues righteousness and loyalty*
> Finds life, righteousness and honor.

31:26 (Of the excellent wife)
> She opens her mouth in wisdom,
> And the teaching of kindness* is on her tongue.

---

*The one Hebrew word *chesed* may be translated into English by "kindness," "lovingkindness," "mercy," "loyalty," and "righteousness." The English versions often vary widely in their choice at any given point.

KNOWLEDGE

(See also "Use of the Proverbs")

1:7

The fear of the Lord is the beginning of knowledge;
Fools despise wisdom and instruction.

1:22,28,29 (Wisdom speaking)

"How long, O naive ones, will you love simplicity?
And scoffers delight themselves in scoffing,
And fools hate knowledge? . . .
[28]"Then they will call on me, but I will not answer;
They will seek me diligently, but they shall not find
me,
[29]Because they hated knowledge,
And did not choose the fear of the Lord."

2:4-6

If you seek her [wisdom] as silver,
And search for her as for hidden treasures;
[5]Then you will discern the fear of the Lord,
And discover the knowledge of God.
[6]For the Lord gives wisdom;
From His mouth come knowledge and understanding.

2:10

For wisdom will enter your heart,
And knowledge will be pleasant to your soul.

3:19,20

The Lord by wisdom founded the earth;

By understanding He established the heavens.
²⁰By his knowledge the deeps were broken up,
And the skies drip with dew.

5:1,2

My son, give attention to my wisdom,
Incline your ear to my understanding;
²That you may observe discretion,
And your lips may reserve knowledge.

8:8-12 (Wisdom speaking)

"All the utterances of my mouth are in
        righteousness;
There is nothing crooked or perverted in them.
⁹"They are all straightforward to him who
        understands,
And right to those who find knowledge.
¹⁰"Take my instruction, and not silver,
And knowledge rather than choicest gold.
¹¹"For wisdom is better than jewels;
And all desirable things cannot compare with her.

¹²"I, wisdom, dwell with prudence,
And I find knowledge and discretion."

9:10

The fear of the LORD is the beginning of wisdom,
And the knowledge of the Holy One is
        understanding.

10:14

Wise men store up knowledge,
But with the mouth of the foolish, ruin is at hand.

11:9

With his mouth the godless man destroys his neighbor,
But through knowledge the righteous will be delivered.

12:1

Whoever loves discipline loves knowledge,
But he who hates reproof is stupid.

12:23

A prudent man conceals knowledge,
But the heart of fools proclaims folly.

13:16

Every prudent man acts with knowledge,
But a fool displays folly.

14:6,7

A scoffer seeks wisdom, and finds none,
But knowledge is easy to him who has
    understanding.
[7]Leave the presence of a fool,
Or you will not discern words of knowledge.

14:18

The naive inherit folly,
But the prudent are crowned with knowledge.

15:2

The tongue of the wise makes knowledge
    acceptable,
But the mouth of fools spouts folly.

15:7

The lips of the wise spread knowledge,
But the hearts of fools are not so.

15:14

The mind of the intelligent seeks knowledge,
But the mouth of fools feeds on folly.

17:27

He who restrains his words has knowledge,
And he who has a cool spirit is a man of
    understanding.

18:15

> The mind of the prudent acquires knowledge,
> And the ear of the wise seeks knowledge.

19:2

> Also it is not good for a person to be without
>   knowledge,
> And he who makes haste with his feet errs.

19:25

> Strike a scoffer and the naive may become shrewd,
> But reprove one who has understanding and he
>   will gain knowledge.

19:27

> Cease listening, my son, to discipline,
> And you will stray from the words of knowledge.

20:15

> There is gold, and an abundance of jewels;
> But the lips of knowledge are a more precious
>   thing.

21:11

> When the scoffer is punished, the naive becomes
>   wise;
> But when the wise is instructed, he receives
>   knowledge.

22:12

> The eyes of the LORD preserve knowledge,
> But He overthrows the words of the treacherous
>   man.

22:17-21

> Incline your ear and hear the words of the wise,
> And apply your mind to my knowledge;
> [18]For it will be pleasant if you keep them within you,

That they may be ready on your lips.
¹⁹So that your trust may be in the LORD,
I have taught you today, even you.
²⁰Have I not written to you excellent things
Of counsels and knowledge,
²¹To make you know the certainty of the words of
truth
That you may correctly answer to him who sent you?

23:12

Apply your heart to discipline,
And your ears to words of knowledge.

24:3-5

By wisdom a house is built,
And by understanding it is established;
⁴And by knowledge the rooms are filled
With all precious and pleasant riches.

⁵A wise man is strong,
And a man of knowledge increases power.

30:1-4

The words of Agur the son of Jakeh, the oracle.
The man declares to Ithiel, to Ithiel and Ucal:
²Surely I am more stupid than any man,
And I do not have the understanding of a man.
³Neither have I learned wisdom,
Nor do I have the knowledge of the Holy One.
⁴Who has ascended into heaven and descended?
Who has gathered the wind in His fists?
Who has wrapped the waters in His garment?
Who has established all the ends of the earth?
What is His name or His son's name?
Surely you know!

LAZINESS

6:6-11

>   Go to the ant, O sluggard,
>   Observe her ways and be wise,
> [7]Which, having no chief,
>   Officer or ruler,
> [8]Prepares her food in the summer,
>   And gathers her provision in the harvest.
> [9]How long will you lie down, O sluggard?
>   When will you arise from your sleep?
> [10]"A little sleep, a little slumber,
>   A little folding of the hands to rest"—
> [11]And your poverty will come in like a vagabond,
>   And your need like an armed man.

10:4,5

>   Poor is he who works with a negligent hand,
>   But the hand of the diligent makes rich.
> [5]He who gathers in summer is a son who acts wisely,
>   But he who sleeps in harvest is a son who acts
>   shamefully.

10:26

>   Like vinegar to the teeth and smoke to the eyes,
>   So is the lazy one to those who send him.

12:24

>   The hand of the diligent will rule,
>   But the slack hand will be put to forced labor.

12:27

>   A slothful man does not roast his prey,
>   But the precious possession of a man is diligence.

13:4

The soul of the sluggard craves and gets nothing,
But the soul of the diligent is made fat.

15:19

The way of the sluggard is as a hedge of thorns,
But the path of the upright is a highway.

19:15

Laziness casts into a deep sleep,
And an idle man will suffer hunger.

19:24

The sluggard buries his hand in the dish,
And will not even bring it back to his mouth.

20:4

The sluggard does not plow after the autumn,
So he begs during the harvest and has nothing.

20:13

Do not love sleep, lest you become poor;
Open your eyes, and you will be satisfied with food.

21:25,26

The desire of the sluggard puts him to death,
For his hands refuse to work;
²⁶All day long he is craving,
While the righteous gives and does not hold back.

22:13

The sluggard says, "There is a lion outside;
I shall be slain in the street!"

24:30-34

I passed by the field of the sluggard,
And by the vineyard of the man lacking sense;
³¹And behold, it was completely overgrown with
    thistles,

Its surface was covered with nettles,
And its stone wall was broken down.
[32]When I saw, I reflected upon it;
I looked, and received instruction.
[33]"A little sleep, a little slumber,
A little folding of the hands to rest,"
[34]Then your poverty will come as a robber,
And your want like an armed man.

26:13-16

The sluggard says, "There is a lion in the road!
A lion is in the open square!"
[14]As the door turns on its hinges,
So does the sluggard on his bed.
[15]The sluggard buries his hand in the dish;
He is weary of bringing it to his mouth again.
[16]The sluggard is wiser in his own eyes
Than seven men who can give a discreet answer.

31:27 (Of the excellent wife)

She looks well to the ways of her household,
And does not eat the bread of idleness.

LOVE

3:12

> . . . whom the LORD loves He reproves,
> Even as a father the son in whom he delights.

5:18,19

> Let your fountain be blessed,
> And rejoice in the wife of your youth.
> ^{19}As a loving hind and a graceful doe,
> Let her breasts satisfy you at all times;
> Be exhilarated always with her love.

7:18-20 (The adulteress speaking)

> "Come, let us drink our fill of love until morning;
> Let us delight ourselves with caresses.
> ^{19}"For the man is not at home,
> He has gone on a long journey;
> ^{20}He has taken a bag of money with him,
> At full moon he will come home."

8:17,20,21 (Wisdom speaking)

> "I love those who love me;
> And those who seek me diligently will find me. . . .
> ^{20}"I walk in the way of righteousness,
> In the midst of the paths of justice,
> ^{21}To endow those who love me with wealth,
> That I may fill their treasuries."

9:8

> Do not reprove a scoffer, lest he hate you,
> Reprove a wise man, and he will love you.

10:12

Hatred stirs up strife,
But love covers all transgressions.

12:1

Whoever loves discipline loves knowledge,
But he who hates reproof is stupid.

13:24

He who spares his rod hates his son,
But he who loves him disciplines him diligently.

14:20

The poor is hated even by his neighbor,
But those who love the rich are many.

15:9

The way of the wicked is an abomination to the LORD,
But He loves him who pursues righteousness.

15:17

Better is a dish of vegetables where love is,
Than a fattened ox and hatred with it.

16:7

When a man's ways are pleasing to the LORD,
He makes even his enemies to be at peace with him.

16:13

Righteous lips are the delight of kings,
And he who speaks right is loved.

17:9

He who covers a transgression seeks love,
But he who repeats a matter separates intimate
    friends.

17:17

A friend loves at all times,
And a brother is born for adversity.

17:19

> He who loves transgression loves strife;
> He who raises his door seeks destruction.

18:24

> A man of many friends comes to ruin,
> But there is a friend who sticks closer than a
>   brother.

19:8

> He who gets wisdom loves his own soul;
> He who keeps understanding will find good.

21:17

> He who loves pleasure will become a poor man;
> He who loves wine and oil will not become rich.

22:11

> He who loves purity of heart
> And whose speech is gracious, the king is his
>   friend.

24:17,18

> Do not rejoice when your enemy falls,
> And do not let your heart be glad when he stumbles;
> [18]Lest the LORD see it and be displeased,
> And He turn away His anger from him.

25:21,22

> If your enemy is hungry, give him food to eat;
> And if he is thirsty, give him water to drink;
> [22]For you will heap burning coals on his head,
> And the LORD will reward you.

27:5,6

> Better is open rebuke
> Than love that is concealed.
> [6]Faithful are the wounds of a friend,
> But deceitful are the kisses of an enemy.

29:3

A man who loves wisdom makes his father glad,
But he who keeps company with harlots wastes his
wealth.

LYING

6:16-19

There are six things which the LORD hates,
Yes, seven which are an abomination to Him:
[17] Haughty eyes, a lying tongue,
And hands that shed innocent blood,
[18] A heart that devises wicked plans,
Feet that run rapidly to evil,
[19] A false witness who utters lies,
And one who spreads strife among brothers.

10:18

He who conceals hatred has lying lips,
And he who spreads slander is a fool.

12:17

He who speaks truth tells what is right,
But a false witness, deceit.

12:19

Truthful lips will be established forever,
But a lying tongue is only for a moment.

12:22

Lying lips are an abomination to the LORD,
But those who deal faithfully are His delight.

13:5

A righteous man hates falsehood,
But a wicked man acts disgustingly and shamefully.

14:5

A faithful witness will not lie,
But a false witness speaks lies.

14:25

A truthful witness saves lives,
But he who speaks lies is treacherous.

17:4

An evildoer listens to wicked lips,
A liar pays attention to a destructive tongue.

17:7

Excellent speech is not fitting for a fool;
Much less are lying lips to a prince.

19:5

A false witness will not go unpunished,
And he who tells lies will not escape.

19:9

A false witness will not go unpunished,
And he who tells lies will perish.

19:22

What is desirable in a man is his kindness,
And it is better to be a poor man than a liar.

20:17

Bread obtained by falsehood is sweet to a man,
But afterward his mouth will be filled with gravel.

21:6

The getting of treasures by a lying tongue
Is a fleeting vapor, the pursuit of death.

21:28

A false witness will perish,
But the man who listens to the truth will speak forever.

25:14

> Like clouds and wind without rain
> Is a man who boasts of his gifts falsely.

25:18

> Like a club and a sword and a sharp arrow
> Is a man who bears false witness against his neighbor.

26:28

> A lying tongue hates those it crushes,
> And a flattering mouth works ruin.

29:12

> If a ruler pays attention to falsehood,
> All his ministers become wicked.

30:5,6

> Every word of God is tested;
> He is a shield to those who take refuge in Him.
> ⁶Do not add to His words
> Lest He reprove you, and you be proved a liar.

30:7,8

> Two things I asked of Thee,
> Do not refuse me before I die:
> ⁸Keep deception and lies far from me,
> Give me neither poverty nor riches. . . .

THE NAIVE*

(See also "Use of the Proverbs")

1:22,23 (Wisdom speaking)

"How long, O naive ones, will you love simplicity?
And scoffers delight themselves in scoffing,
And fools hate knowledge?
²³ "Turn to my reproof,
Behold, I will pour out my spirit on you;
I will make my words known to you. . . ."

1:32,33 (Wisdom speaking)

"For the waywardness of the naive shall kill them,
And the complacency of fools shall destroy them.
³³ "But he who listens to me shall live securely,
And shall be at ease from the dread of evil."

7:6-23

For at the window of my house
I looked out through my lattice,
⁷And I saw among the naive,
I discerned among the youths,
A young man lacking sense,
⁸Passing through the street near her corner;
And he takes the way to her house,
⁹In the twilight, in the evening,
In the middle of the night and in the darkness.
¹⁰And behold, a woman comes to meet him,

---

*May also be translated "the simple."

Dressed as a harlot and cunning of heart.
¹¹She is boisterous and rebellious;
   Her feet do not remain at home;
¹²She is now in the streets, now in the squares,
   And lurks by every corner.
¹³So she seizes him and kisses him,
   And with a brazen face she says to him:
¹⁴"I was due to offer peace offerings;
   Today I have paid my vows.
¹⁵"Therefore I have come out to meet you,
   To seek your presence earnestly, and I have found
      you.
¹⁶"I have spread my couch with coverings,
   With colored linens of Egypt.
¹⁷"I have sprinkled my bed
   With myrrh, aloes and cinnamon.
¹⁸"Come, let us drink our fill of love until morning;
   Let us delight ourselves with caresses.
¹⁹"For the man is not at home,
   He has gone on a long journey;
²⁰He has taken a bag of money with him
   At full moon he will come home."
²¹With her many persuasions she entices him;
   With her flattering lips she seduces him.
²²Suddenly he follows her,
   As an ox goes to the slaughter,
   Or as one in fetters to the discipline of a fool,
²³Until an arrow pierces through his liver;
   As a bird hastens to the snare,
   So he does not know that it will cost him his life.

8:5,6 (Wisdom speaking)
   "O naive ones, discern prudence;
   And, O fools, discern wisdom.

⁶"Listen, for I shall speak noble things;
   And the opening of my lips shall produce right
      things."

9:4-6 (Wisdom speaking)
   "Whoever is naive, let him turn in here!"
   To him who lacks understanding she says,
⁵"Come, eat of my food,
   And drink of the wine I have mixed.
⁶"Forsake your folly and live,
   And proceed in the way of understanding."

14:15

   The naive believes everything,
   But the prudent man considers his steps.

14:18

   The naive inherit folly,
   But the prudent are crowned with knowledge.

19:25

   Strike a scoffer and the naive may become shrewd,
   But reprove one who has understanding and he
      will gain knowledge.

21:11

   When the scoffer is punished, the naive becomes
      wise;
   But when the wise is instructed, he receives
      knowledge.

22:3

   The prudent sees the evil and hides himself,
   But the naive go on, and are punished for it.

27:12

   A prudent man sees evil and hides himself,
   The naive proceed and pay the penalty.

PARENTS

1:8,9

> Hear, my son, your father's instruction,
> And do not forsake your mother's teaching;
> [9]Indeed, they are a graceful wreath to your head,
> And ornaments about your neck.

3:1,2

> My son, do not forget my teaching,
> But let your heart keep my commandments;
> [2]For length of days and years of life,
> And peace they will add to you.

4:1-6

> Hear, O sons, the instruction of a father,
> And give attention that you may gain understanding,
> [2]For I give you sound teaching;
> Do not abandon my instruction.
> [3]When I was a son to my father,
> Tender and the only son in the sight of my mother,
> [4]Then he taught me and said to me,
> "Let your heart hold fast my words;
> Keep my commandments and live;
> [5]Acquire wisdom! Acquire understanding!
> Do not forget, nor turn away from the words of my
> mouth.
> [6]"Do not forsake her, and she will guard you;
> Love her, and she will watch over you."

6:20-24

My son, observe the commandment of your father,
And do not forsake the teaching of your mother;
^{21}Bind them continually on your heart;
Tie them around your neck.
^{22}When you walk about, they will guide you;
When you sleep, they will watch over you;
And when you awake, they will talk to you.
^{23}For the commandment is a lamp, and the teaching
is light;
And reproofs for discipline are the way of life,
^{24}To keep you from the evil woman,
From the smooth tongue of the adulteress.

10:1

A wise son makes a father glad,
But a foolish son is a grief to his mother.

13:1

A wise son accepts his father's discipline,
But a scoffer does not listen to rebuke.

15:5

A fool rejects his father's discipline,
But he who regards reproof is prudent.

15:20

A wise son makes a father glad,
But a foolish man despises his mother.

17:6

Grandchildren are the crown of old men,
And the glory of sons is their fathers.

17:21

He who begets a fool does so to his sorrow,
And the father of a fool has no joy.

17:25

> A foolish son is a grief to his father,
> And bitterness to her who bore him.

19:13,14

> A foolish son is destruction to his father,
> And the contentions of a wife are a constant dripping.
> ¹⁴House and wealth are an inheritance from fathers,
> But a prudent wife is from the LORD.

19:26

> He who assaults his father and drives his mother
>   away
> Is a shameful and disgraceful son.

20:7

> A righteous man who walks in his integrity—
> How blessed are his sons after him.

20:20

> He who curses his father or his mother,
> His lamp will go out in time of darkness.

22:6

> Train up a child in the way he should go,
> Even when he is old he will not depart from it.

23:22-25

> Listen to your father who begot you,
> And do not despise your mother when she is old.
> ²³Buy truth, and do not sell it,
> Get wisdom and instruction and understanding.
>
> ²⁴The father of the righteous will greatly rejoice,
> And he who begets a wise son will be glad in him.
> ²⁵Let your father and your mother be glad,
> And let her rejoice who gave birth to you.

27:11

Be wise, my son, and make my heart glad,
That I may reply to him who reproaches me.

28:7

He who keeps the law is a discerning son,
But he who is a companion of gluttons humiliates
   his father.

28:24

He who robs his father or his mother,
And says, "It is not a transgression,"
Is the companion of a man who destroys.

29:3

A man who loves wisdom makes his father glad,
But he who keeps company with harlots wastes his
   wealth.

29:15

The rod and reproof give wisdom,
But a child who gets his own way brings shame to
   his mother.

30:11

There is a kind of man who curses his father,
And does not bless his mother.

30:17

The eye that mocks a father,
And scorns a mother,
The ravens of the valley will pick it out,
And the young eagles will eat it.

PLANS

15:22

Without consultation, plans are frustrated,
But with many counselors they succeed.

15:26

Evil plans are an abomination to the LORD,
But pleasant words are pure.

16:1

The plans of the heart belong to man,
But the answer of the tongue is from the LORD.

16:3

Commit your works to the LORD,
And your plans will be established.

16:9

The mind of man plans his way,
But the LORD directs his steps.

16:30

He who winks his eyes does so to devise perverse
things;
He who compresses his lips brings evil to pass.

19:21

Many are the plans in a man's heart,
But the counsel of the LORD, it will stand.

20:5

A plan in the heart of a man is like deep water,
But a man of understanding draws it out.

20:18

Prepare plans by consultation,
And make war by wise guidance.

21:5

The plans of the diligent lead surely to advantage,
But everyone who is hasty comes surely to poverty.

24:8,9

He who plans to do evil,
Men will call him a schemer.
[9]The devising of folly is sin,
And the scoffer is an abomination to men.

POLITICAL LEADERS

8:14-16 (Wisdom speaking)

"Counsel is mine and sound wisdom;
I am understanding, power is mine.
¹⁵"By me kings reign,
And rulers decree justice.
¹⁶"By me princes rule, and nobles,
All who judge rightly."

14:28

In a multitude of people is a king's glory,
But in the dearth of people is a prince's ruin.

14:34,35

Righteousness exalts a nation,
But sin is a disgrace to any people.
³⁵The king's favor is toward a servant who acts wisely,
But his anger is toward him who acts shamefully.

16:10

A divine decision is in the lips of the king;
His mouth should not err in judgment.

16:12-15

It is an abomination for kings to commit
wickedness,
For a throne is established on righteousness.
¹³Righteous lips are the delight of kings,
And he who speaks right is loved.
¹⁴The wrath of a king is as messengers of death,
But a wise man will appease it.

¹⁵In the light of a king's face is life,
And his favor is like a cloud with the spring rain.

17:7

Excellent speech is not fitting for a fool;
Much less are lying lips to a prince.

19:10

Luxury is not fitting for a fool;
Much less for a slave to rule over princes.

19:12

The king's wrath is like the roaring of a lion,
But his favor is like dew on the grass.

20:2

The terror of a king is like the growling of a lion;
He who provokes him to anger forfeits his own life.

20:8

A king who sits on the throne of justice
Disperses all evil with his eyes.

20:26

A wise king winnows the wicked,
And drives the threshing-wheel over them.

20:28

Loyalty and truth preserve the king,
And he upholds his throne by righteousness.

21:1

The king's heart is like channels of water in the
hand of the LORD;
He turns it wherever He wishes.

22:11

He who loves purity of heart
And whose speech is gracious, the king is his friend.

22:29

> Do you see a man skilled in his work?
> He will stand before kings;
> He will not stand before obscure men.

23:1-3

> When you sit down to dine with a ruler,
> Consider carefully what is before you;
> ²And put a knife to your throat,
> If you are a man of great appetite.
> ³Do not desire his delicacies,
> For it is deceptive food.

24:21,22

> My son, fear the LORD and the king;
> Do not associate with those who are given to
>   change;
> ²²For their calamity will rise suddenly,
> And who knows the ruin that comes from both of
>   them?

25:2-7

> It is the glory of God to conceal a matter,
> But the glory of kings is to search out a matter.
> ³As the heavens for height and the earth for depth,
> So the heart of kings is unsearchable.
> ⁴Take away the dross from the silver,
> And there comes out a vessel for the smith;
> ⁵Take away the wicked from before the king,
> And his throne will be established in righteousness.
> ⁶Do not claim honor in the presence of the king,
> And do not stand in the place of great men;
> ⁷For it is better that it be said of you, "Come up
>   here,"

Than that you should be put lower in the presence
of the prince,
Whom your eyes have seen.

28:2

By the transgression of a land many are its princes,
But by a man of understanding and knowledge, so
it endures.

28:15,16

Like a roaring lion and rushing bear
Is a wicked ruler over a poor people.
[16]A leader who is a great oppressor lacks
understanding,
But he who hates unjust gain will prolong his days.

29:2

When the righteous increase, the people rejoice,
But when a wicked man rules, people groan.

29:4

The king gives stability to the land by justice,
But a man who takes bribes overthrows it.

29:12

If a ruler pays attention to falsehood,
All his ministers become wicked.

29:14

If a king judges the poor with truth,
His throne will be established forever.

29:26

Many seek the ruler's favor,
But justice for man comes from the LORD.

30:29-31

There are three things which are stately in their
march,

Even four which are stately when they walk:
³⁰The lion which is mighty among beasts
And does not retreat before any,
³¹The strutting cock, the male goat also,
And a king when his army is with him.

31:1-9

The words of King Lemuel, the oracle which his
mother taught him.
²What, O my son?
And what, O son of my womb?
And what, O son of my vows?
³Do not give your strength to women,
Or your ways to that which destroys kings.
⁴It is not for kings, O Lemuel,
It is not for kings to drink wine,
Or for rulers to desire strong drink.
⁵Lest they drink and forget what is decreed,
And pervert the rights of all the afflicted.
⁶Give strong drink to him who is perishing,
And wine to him whose life is bitter.
⁷Let him drink and forget his poverty,
And remember his trouble no more.
⁸Open your mouth for the dumb,
For the rights of all the unfortunate.
⁹Open your mouth, judge righteously,
And defend the rights of the afflicted and needy.

THE POOR

3:34

Though He scoffs at the scoffers,
Yet He gives grace to the afflicted.

10:4

Poor is he who works with a negligent hand,
But the hand of the diligent makes rich.

10:15

The rich man's wealth is his fortress,
The ruin of the poor is their poverty.

13:7,8

There is one who pretends to be rich, but has
    nothing;
Another pretends to be poor, but has great wealth.
[8]The ransom of a man's life is his riches,
But the poor hears no rebuke.

13:23

Abundant food is in the fallow ground of the
    poor,
But it is swept away by injustice.

14:20,21

The poor is hated even by his neighbor,
But those who love the rich are many.
[21]He who despises his neighbor sins,
But happy is he who is gracious to the poor.

14:31

He who oppresses the poor reproaches his Maker,
But he who is gracious to the needy honors Him.

15:15

All the days of the afflicted are bad,
But a cheerful heart has a continual feast.

16:19

It is better to be of a humble spirit with the lowly,
Than to divide the spoil with the proud.

17:5

He who mocks the poor reproaches his Maker;
He who rejoices at calamity will not go unpunished.

18:23

The poor man utters supplications,
But the rich man answers roughly.

19:1

Better is a poor man who walks in his integrity
Than he who is perverse in speech and is a fool.

19:4

Wealth adds many friends,
But a poor man is separated from his friend.

19:7

All the brothers of a poor man hate him;
How much more do his friends go far from him!
He pursues them with words, but they are gone.

19:17

He who is gracious to a poor man lends to the
    Lord,
And He will repay him for his good deed.

19:22

What is desirable in a man is his kindness,

And it is better to be a poor man than a liar.

21:13

He who shuts his ear to the cry of the poor
Will also cry himself and not be answered.

21:17

He who loves pleasure will become a poor man;
He who loves wine and oil will not become rich.

22:2

The rich and the poor have a common bond,
The LORD is the maker of them all.

22:7

The rich rules over the poor,
And the borrower becomes the lender's slave.

22:9

He who is generous will be blessed,
For he gives some of his food to the poor.

22:16

He who oppresses the poor to make much for
    himself
Or who gives to the rich, will only come to
    poverty.

22:22,23

Do not rob the poor because he is poor,
Or crush the afflicted at the gate;
[23] For the LORD will plead their case,
And take the life of those who rob them.

28:3

A poor man who oppresses the lowly
Is like a driving rain which leaves no food.

28:6

Better is the poor who walks in his integrity,

Than he who is crooked though he be rich.

28:8

He who increases his wealth by interest and usury,
Gathers it for him who is gracious to the poor.

28:11

The rich man is wise in his own eyes,
But the poor who has understanding sees through
  him.

28:15

Like a roaring lion and a rushing bear
Is a wicked ruler over a poor people.

28:27

He who gives to the poor will never want,
But he who shuts his eyes will have many curses.

29:7

The righteous is concerned for the rights of the poor,
The wicked does not understand such concern.

29:13,14

The poor man and the oppressor have this in
  common:
The LORD gives light to the eyes of both.
[14] If a king judges the poor with truth,
His throne will be established forever.

30:14

There is a kind of man whose teeth are like swords,
And his jaw teeth like knives,
To devour the afflicted from the earth,
And the needy from among men.

31:1,8,9

The words of King Lemuel, the oracle which his
  mother taught him. . . .

⁸Open your mouth for the dumb,
For the rights of all the unfortunate.
⁹Open your mouth, judge righteously,
And defend the rights of the afflicted and needy.

31:20 (Of the excellent wife)
She extends her hand to the poor;
And she stretches out her hands to the needy.

PRAYER

15:8

> The sacrifice of the wicked is an abomination to the
> Lord,
> But the prayer of the upright is His delight.

15:29

> The Lord is far from the wicked,
> But He hears the prayer of the righteous.

20:25

> It is a snare for a man to say rashly, "It is holy!"
> And after the vows to make inquiry.

28:9

> He who turns away his ear from listening to the law,
> Even his prayer is an abomination.

28:13

> He who conceals his transgressions will not
> prosper,
> But he who confesses and forsakes them will find
> compassion.

PRIDE

8:13b (Wisdom speaking)
"Pride and arrogance and the evil way,
And the perverted mouth, I hate."

11:2

When pride comes, then comes dishonor,
But with the humble is wisdom.

15:25

The LORD will tear down the house of the proud,
But He will establish the boundary of the widow.

16:5

Everyone who is proud in heart is an abomination
    to the LORD;
Assuredly, he will not be unpunished.

16:18,19

Pride goes before destruction,
And a haughty spirit before stumbling.
¹⁹It is better to be of a humble spirit with the lowly,
Than to divide the spoil with the proud.

18:12

Before destruction the heart of man is haughty,
But humility goes before honor.

21:4

Haughty eyes and a proud heart,
The lamp of the wicked, is sin.

21:24

"Proud," "Haughty," "Scoffer," are his names,
Who acts with insolent pride.

28:25

> An arrogant man stirs up strife,
> But he who trusts in the LORD will prosper.

29:23

> A man's pride will bring him low,
> But a humble spirit will obtain honor.

30:13

> There is a kind—oh how lofty are his eyes!
> And his eyelids are raised in arrogance.

PROTECTION

2:7,8

He [the Lord] stores up sound wisdom for the
upright;
He is a shield to those who walk in integrity,
⁸Guarding the paths of justice,
And He preserves the way of His godly ones.

3:25,26

Do not be afraid of sudden fear,
Nor the onslaught of the wicked when it comes;
²⁶For the Lord will be your confidence,
And will keep your foot from being caught.

10:24,25

What the wicked fears will come upon him,
And the desire of the righteous will be granted.
²⁵When the whirlwind passes, the wicked is no more,
But the righteous has an everlasting foundation.

10:29,30

The way of the Lord is a stronghold to the upright,
But ruin to the workers of iniquity.
³⁰The righteous will never be shaken,
But the wicked will not dwell in the land.

11:8

The righteous is delivered from trouble,
But the wicked takes his place.

12:21

No harm befalls the righteous,
But the wicked are filled with trouble.

14:26

> In the fear of the LORD there is strong confidence,
> And his children will have refuge.

14:32

> The wicked is thrust down by his wrong-doing,
> But the righteous has a refuge when he dies.

15:3

> The eyes of the LORD are in every place,
> Watching the evil and the good.

18:10

> The name of the LORD is a strong tower;
> The righteous runs into it and is safe.

19:16

> He who keeps the commandment keeps his soul,
> But he who is careless of his ways will die.

22:3

> The prudent sees the evil and hides himself,
> But the naive go on, and are punished for it.

22:5

> Thorns and snares are in the way of the perverse;
> He who guards himself will be far from them.

30:5

> Every word of God is tested;
> He is a shield to those who take refuge in Him.

THE RIGHTEOUS

A. General

2:7

He [the LORD] stores up sound wisdom for the
  upright;
He is a shield to those who walk in integrity.

9:9

Give instruction to a wise man, and he will be still
  wiser,
Teach a righteous man, and he will increase his
  learning.

11:30

The fruit of the righteous is a tree of life,
And he who is wise wins souls.

16:17

The highway of the upright is to depart from evil;
He who watches his way preserves his life.

17:26

It is also not good to fine the righteous,
Nor to strike the noble for their uprightness.

18:10

The name of the LORD is a strong tower;
The righteous runs into it and is safe.

20:7

A righteous man who walks in his integrity—
How blessed are his sons after him.

23:24

> The father of the righteous will greatly rejoice,
> And he who begets a wise son will be glad in him.

28:10

> He who leads the upright astray in an evil way
> Will himself fall into his own pit,
> But the blameless will inherit good.

B. *The Righteous versus the Wicked, the Sinner, the Fool, etc.*

2:21,22

> . . . the upright will live in the land,
> And the blameless will remain in it;
> [22]But the wicked will be cut off from the land,
> And the treacherous will be uprooted from it.

3:32,33

> . . . the crooked man is an abomination to the
>   LORD;
> But He is intimate with the upright.
> [33]The curse of the LORD is on the house of the wicked,
> But he blesses the dwelling of the righteous.

4:18,19

> . . . the path of the righteous is like the light of dawn,
> That shines brighter and brighter until the full day.
> [19]The way of the wicked is like darkness;
> They do not know over what they stumble.

10:3

> The LORD will not allow the righteous to hunger,
> But he will thrust aside the craving of the wicked.

10:6,7

> Blessings are on the head of the righteous,
> But the mouth of the wicked conceals violence.

⁷The memory of the righteous is blessed,
But the name of the wicked will rot.

10:11

The mouth of the righteous is a fountain of life,
But the mouth of the wicked conceals violence.

10:16

The wages of the righteous is life,
The income of the wicked, punishment.

10:20,21

The tongue of the righteous is as choice silver,
The heart of the wicked is worth little.
²¹The lips of the righteous feed many,
But fools die for lack of understanding.

10:24,25

What the wicked fears will come upon him,
And the desire of the righteous will be granted.
²⁵When the whirlwind passes, the wicked is no more,
But the righteous has an everlasting foundation.

10:28-32

The hope of the righteous is gladness,
But the expectation of the wicked perishes.
²⁹The way of the LORD is a stronghold to the upright,
But ruin to the workers of iniquity.
³⁰The righteous will never be shaken,
But the wicked will not dwell in the land.
³¹The mouth of the righteous flows with
    wisdom,
But the perverted tongue will be cut out.
³²The lips of the righteous bring forth what is
    acceptable,
But the mouth of the wicked, what is perverted.

11:3-11

The integrity of the upright will guide them,
But the falseness of the treacherous will destroy
them.
[4]Riches do not profit in the day of wrath,
But righteousness delivers from death.
[5]The righteousness of the blameless will smooth his
way,
But the wicked will fall by his own wickedness.
[6]The righteousness of the upright will deliver them,
But the treacherous will be caught by their own
greed.
[7]When a wicked man dies, his expectation will perish,
And the hope of the strong men perishes.
[8]The righteous is delivered from trouble,
But the wicked takes his place.
[9]With his mouth the godless man destroys his
neighbor,
But through knowledge the righteous will be
delivered.
[10]When it goes well with the righteous, the city rejoices,
And when the wicked perish, there is glad shouting.
[11]By the blessing of the upright a city is exalted,
But by the mouth of the wicked it is torn down.

11:18

The wicked earns deceptive wages,
But he who sows righteousness gets a true reward.

11:21

Assuredly, the evil man will not go unpunished,
But the descendants of the righteous will be
delivered.

11:23

The desire of the righteous is only good,

But the expectation of the wicked is wrath.

11:28

He who trusts in his riches will fall,
But the righteous will flourish like the green leaf.

11:30,31

The fruit of the righteous is a tree of life,
And he who is wise wins souls.
[31]If the righteous will be rewarded in the earth,
How much more the wicked and the sinner!

12:3

A man will not be established by wickedness,
But the root of the righteous will not be moved.

12:5-7

The thoughts of the righteous are just,
But the counsels of the wicked are deceitful.
[6]The words of the wicked lie in wait for blood,
But the mouth of the upright will deliver them.
[7]The wicked are overthrown and are no more,
But the house of the righteous will stand.

12:10

A righteous man has regard for the life of his beast,
But the compassion of the wicked is cruel.

12:12,13

The wicked desires the booty of evil men,
But the root of the righteous yields fruit.
[13]An evil man is ensnared by the transgression of his
lips,
But the righteous will escape from trouble.

12:21

No harm befalls the righteous,
But the wicked are filled with trouble.

12:26

> The righteous is a guide to his neighbor,
> But the way of the wicked leads them astray.

13:5,6

> A righteous man hates falsehood,
> But a wicked man acts disgustingly and
>   shamefully.
> ⁶Righteousness guards the one whose way is
>   blameless,
> But wickedness subverts the sinner.

13:9

> The light of the righteous rejoices,
> But the lamp of the wicked goes out.

13:21,22

> Adversity pursues sinners,
> But the righteous will be rewarded with prosperity.
> ²²A good man leaves an inheritance to his children's
>   children,
> And the wealth of the sinner is stored up for the
>   righteous.

13:25

> The righteous has enough to satisfy his appetite,
> But the stomach of the wicked is in want.

14:9

> Fools mock at sin,
> But among the upright there is good will.

14:11

> The house of the wicked will be destroyed,
> But the tent of the upright will flourish.

14:19

> The evil will bow down before the good,

And the wicked at the gates of the righteous.

14:32

The wicked is thrust down by his wrong-doing,
But the righteous has a refuge when he dies.

15:6

Much wealth is in the house of the righteous,
But trouble is in the income of the wicked.

15:8,9

The sacrifice of the wicked is an abomination to the
Lord,
But the prayer of the upright is His delight.
⁹The way of the wicked is an abomination to the
Lord,
But he loves him who pursues righteousness.

15:19

The way of the sluggard is a hedge of thorns,
But the path of the upright is a highway.

15:28,29

The heart of the righteous ponders how to answer,
But the mouth of the wicked pours out evil things.
²⁹The Lord is far from the wicked,
But He hears the prayer of the righteous.

18:5

To show partiality to the wicked is not good,
Nor to thrust aside the righteous in judgment.

21:12

The righteous one considers the house of the
wicked,
Turning the wicked to ruin.

21:15

The execution of justice is joy for the righteous,

But is terror to the workers of iniquity.

21:18

The wicked is a ransom for the righteous,
And the treacherous is in the place of the upright.

21:25,26

The desire of the sluggard puts him to death,
For his hands refuse to work;
[26] All day long he is craving,
While the righteous gives and does not hold back.

21:29

A wicked man shows a bold face,
But as for the upright, he makes his way sure.

24:15,16

Do not lie in wait, O wicked man, against the
    dwelling of the righteous;
Do not destroy his resting place;
[16] For a righteous man falls seven times,
    and rises again,
But the wicked stumble in time of calamity.

25:26

Like a trampled spring and a polluted well
Is a righteous man who gives way before the wicked.

28:1

The wicked flee when no one is pursuing,
But the righteous are bold as a lion.

28:12

When the righteous triumph, there is great glory,
But when the wicked rise, men hide themselves.

28:28

When the wicked rise, men hide themselves;
But when they perish, the righteous increase.

29:2

When the righteous increase, the people rejoice,
But when a wicked man rules, people groan.

29:6,7

By transgression an evil man is ensnared,
But the righteous sings and rejoices.
⁷The righteous is concerned for the rights of the
poor,
The wicked does not understand such concern.

29:10

Men of bloodshed hate the blameless,
But the upright are concerned for his life.

29:16

When the wicked increase, transgression increases;
But the righteous will see their fall.

29:27

An unjust man is abominable to the righteous,
And he who is upright in the way is abominable to
the wicked.

RIGHTEOUSNESS*

(See also "Use of the Proverbs")

2:7-9

He [the LORD] stores up sound wisdom for the
    upright:
He is a shield to those who walk in integrity,
[8]Guarding the paths of justice,
And He preserves the way of His godly ones.
[9]Then you will discern righteousness and justice
And equity and every good course.

8:8 (Wisdom speaking)

"All the utterances of my mouth are in
    righteousness;
There is nothing crooked or perverted in them."

8:15-21 (Wisdom speaking)

"By me kings reign,
And rulers decree justice.
[16]"By me princes rule, and nobles,
All who judge rightly.
[17]"I love those who love me;
And those who diligently seek me will find me.
[18]"Riches and honor are with me,
Enduring wealth and righteousness.
[19]"My fruit is better than gold, even pure gold,
And my yield than choicest silver.

———

*This may also be translated "justice" (see 8:15).

^{20}"I walk in the way of righteousness,
In the midst of the paths of justice,

^{21}To endow those who love me with wealth,
That I may fill their treasuries."

10:2

Ill-gotten gains do not profit,
But righteousness delivers from death.

11:4-6

Riches do not profit in the day of wrath,
But righteousness delivers from death.
^{5}The righteousness of the blameless will smooth his
way,
But the wicked will fall by his own wickedness.
^{6}The righteousness of the upright will deliver them,
But the treacherous will be caught by their own
greed.

11:18,19

The wicked earns deceptive wages,
But he who sows righteousness gets a true reward.
^{19}He who is steadfast in righteousness will attain to life,
And he who pursues evil will bring about his own
death.

12:28

In the way of righteousness is life,
And in its pathway there is no death.

13:6

Righteousness guards the one whose way is
blameless,
But wickedness subverts the sinner.

14:34

Righteousness exalts a nation,
But sin is a disgrace to any people.

15:9

The way of the wicked is an abomination to the
 LORD.
But He loves him who pursues righteousness.

16:8

Better is a little with righteousness
Then great income with injustice.

16:12, 13

It is an abomination for kings to commit
 wickedness.
For a throne is established on righteousness.
[13]Righteous lips are the delight of kings.
And he who speaks right is loved.

16:31

A gray head is a crown of glory:
It is found in the way of righteousness.

21:3

To do righteousness and justice
Is desired by the LORD rather than sacrifice.

21:21

He who pursues righteousness and loyalty
Finds life, righteousness and honor.

25:5

Take away the wicked from before the king,
And his throne will be established in righteousness.

31:9 (To King Lemuel)

Open your mouth, judge righteously,
And defend the rights of the afflicted and needy.

SCOFFERS

1:22 (Wisdom speaking)

"How long, O naive ones, will you love simplicity?
And scoffers delight themselves in scoffing,
And fools hate knowledge?"

3:34

Though He scoffs at the scoffers,
Yet He gives grace to the afflicted.

9:7,8

He who corrects a scoffer gets dishonor for himself,
And he who reproves a wicked man gets insults for
himself.
[8]Do not reprove a scoffer, lest he hate you,
Reprove a wise man, and he will love you.

9:12

If you are wise, you are wise for yourself,
And if you scoff, you alone will bear it.

13:1

A wise son accepts his father's discipline,
But a scoffer does not listen to rebuke.

14:6

A scoffer seeks wisdom, and finds none,
But knowledge is easy to him who has
understanding.

14:9

Fools mock at sin,
But among the upright there is good will.

15:12

A scoffer does not love one who reproves him,
He will not go to the wise.

19:25

Strike a scoffer and the naive may become shrewd,
But reprove one who has understanding and he
will gain knowledge.

19:29

Judgments are prepared for scoffers,
And blows for the back of fools.

21:11

When the scoffer is punished, the naive becomes
wise;
But when the wise is instructed, he receives
knowledge.

21:24

"Proud," "Haughty," "Scoffer," are his names,
Who acts with insolent pride.

22:10

Drive out the scoffer, and contention will go out,
Even strife and dishonor will cease.

24:9

The devising of folly is sin,
And the scoffer is an abomination to men.

29:8

Scorners set a city aflame,
But wise men turn away anger.

SELF-CONTROL

14:17

A quick-tempered man acts foolishly,
And a man of evil devices is hated.

14:29,30

He who is slow to anger has great understanding,
But he who is quick-tempered exalts folly.
³⁰A tranquil heart is life to the body,
But passion is rottenness to the bones.

15:18

A hot-tempered man stirs up strife,
But the slow to anger pacifies contention.

16:32

He who is slow to anger is better than the mighty,
And he who rules his spirit, than he who captures a
city.

17:14

The beginning of strife is like letting out water,
So abandon the quarrel before it breaks out.

17:27,28

He who restrains his words has knowledge,
And he who has a cool spirit is a man of
understanding.
²⁸Even a fool, when he keeps silent, is considered
wise;
When he closes his lips, he is counted prudent.

19:11

A man's discretion makes him slow to anger,

And it is his glory to overlook a transgression.

19:19

A man of great anger shall bear the penalty,
For if you rescue him, you will only have to do it
again.

20:3

Keeping away from strife is an honor for a man,
But any fool will quarrel.

21:23

He who guards his mouth and his tongue,
Guards his soul from troubles.

22:24,25

Do not associate with a man given to anger;
Or go with a hot-tempered man.
²⁵Lest you learn his ways,
And find a snare for yourself.

25:28

Like a city that is broken into and without walls
Is a man who has no control over his spirit.

29:8

Scorners set a city aflame,
But wise men turn away anger.

29:11

A fool always loses his temper,
But a wise man holds it back.

29:20

Do you see a man who is hasty in his words?
There is more hope for a fool than for him.

29:22

An angry man stirs up strife,
And a hot-tempered man abounds in trangression.

30:32,33

>   If you have been foolish in exalting yourself
>   Or if you have plotted evil, put your hand on your
>   mouth.
> [33] For the churning of milk produces butter,
>   And pressing the nose brings forth blood;
>   So the churning of anger produces strife.

SPEECH

(See also "Lying")

2:6

   . . . the Lord gives wisdom;
From His mouth comes knowledge and
   understanding.

4:24

Put away from you a deceitful mouth,
And put devious lips far from you.

5:1-4

My son, give attention to my wisdom,
Incline your ear to my understanding;
[2]That you may observe discretion,
And your lips may reserve knowledge.
[3]For the lips of an adulteress drip honey,
And smoother than oil is her speech;
[4]But in the end she is bitter as wormwood,
Sharp as a two-edged sword.

6:12

A worthless person, a wicked man,
Is the one who walks with a false mouth . .

8:6-9 (Wisdom speaking)

"Listen, for I shall speak noble things;
And the opening of my lips will produce right
   things.
[7]"For my mouth will utter truth;
And wickedness is an abomination to my lips.
[8]"All the utterances of my mouth are in
   righteousness;
There is nothing crooked or perverted in them.

⁹"They are all straightforward to him who
   understands,
And right to those who find knowledge."

10:11

The mouth of the righteous is a fountain of life,
But the mouth of the wicked conceals violence.

10:13,14

On the lips of the discerning, wisdom is found,
But a rod is for the back of him who lacks
   understanding.
¹⁴Wise men store up knowledge,
But with the mouth of the foolish, ruin is at hand.

10:18-21

He who conceals hatred has lying lips,
And he who spreads slander is a fool.
¹⁹When there are many words, transgression is
   unavoidable,
But he who restrains his lips is wise.
²⁰The tongue of the righteous is as choice silver,
The heart of the wicked is worth little.
²¹The lips of the righteous feed many,
But fools die for lack of understanding.

10:31,32

The mouth of the righteous flows with wisdom,
But the perverted tongue will be cut out.
³²The lips of the righteous bring forth what is
   acceptable,
But the mouth of the wicked, what is perverted.

11:9

With his mouth the godless man destroys his neighbor,
But through knowledge the righteous will be
   delivered.

11:11-13

By the blessing of the upright a city is exalted,
But by the mouth of the wicked it is torn down.
[12] He who despises his neighbor lacks sense,
But a man of understanding keeps silent.
[13] He who goes about as a talebearer reveals secrets,
But he who is trustworthy conceals a matter.

12:6

The words of the wicked lie in wait for blood,
But the mouth of the upright will deliver them.

12:13,14

An evil man is ensnared by the transgression of his
lips,
But the righteous will escape from trouble.
[14] A man will be satisfied with good by the fruit of his
words,
And the deeds of a man's hands will return to him.

12:18

There is one who speaks rashly like the thrusts of a
sword,
But the tongue of the wise brings healing.

12:25

Anxiety in the heart of a man weighs it down,
But a good word makes it glad.

13:2,3

From the fruit of a man's mouth he enjoys good,
But the desire of the treacherous is violence.
[3] The one who guards his mouth preserves his
life;
The one who opens wide his lips comes to ruin.

14:3

In the mouth of the foolish is a rod for his back,

But the lips of the wise will preserve them.

14:23

In all labor there is profit,
But mere talk leads only to poverty.

15:1,2

A gentle answer turns away wrath,
But a harsh word stirs up anger.
²The tongue of the wise makes knowledge acceptable
But the mouth of fools spouts folly.

15:4

A soothing tongue is a tree of life,
But perversion in it crushes the spirit.

15:7

The lips of the wise spread knowledge,
But the hearts of fools are not so.

15:23

A man has joy in an apt answer,
And how delightful is a timely word!

15:26

Evil plans are an abomination to the LORD,
But pleasant words are pure.

15:28

The heart of the righteous ponders how to answer,
But the mouth of the wicked pours out evil things.

16:1

The plans of the heart belong to man,
But the answer of the tongue is from the LORD.

16:10

A divine decision is in the lips of the king;
His mouth should not err in judgment.

16:13

Righteous lips are the delight of kings.
And he who speaks right is loved.

16:21

The wise in heart will be called discerning.
And sweetness of speech increases persuasiveness.

16:23,24

The heart of the wise teaches his mouth.
And adds persuasiveness to his lips.
[24] Pleasant words are a honeycomb.
Sweet to the soul and healing to the bones.

16:27,28

A worthless man digs up evil.
While his words are as a scorching fire.
[28] A perverse man spreads strife.
And a slanderer separates intimate friends.

17:4

An evildoer listens to wicked lips.
A liar pays attention to a destructive tongue.

17:7

Excellent speech is not fitting for a fool;
Much less are lying lips to a prince.

17:9

He who covers a transgression seeks love.
But he who repeats a matter separates intimate
    friends.

17:20

He who has a crooked mind finds no good.
And he who is perverted in his language falls into
    evil.

17:27,28

> He who restrains his words has
>> knowledge.
> And he who has a cool spirit is a man of
>> understanding.
> ^{28}Even a fool. when he keeps silent. is considered
>> wise:
> When he closes his lips. he is counted prudent.

18:4

> The words of a man's mouth are deep waters:
> The fountain of wisdom is a bubbling brook.

18:6-8

> A fool's lips bring strife.
> And his mouth calls for blows.
> ^{7}A fool's mouth is his ruin.
> And his lips are the snare of his soul.
> ^{8}The words of a whisperer are like dainty morsels.
> And they go down into the innermost parts of the
>> body.

18:13

> He who gives an answer before he hears.
> It is folly and shame to him.

18:20,21

> With the fruit of a man's mouth his stomach will be
>> satisfied:
> He will be satisfied with the product of his lips.
> ^{21}Death and life are in the power of the tongue,
> And those who love it will eat its fruit.

19:1

> Better is a poor man who walks in his integrity
> Than he who is perverse in speech and is a fool.

19:28

> A rascally witness makes a mockery of justice,

And the mouth of the wicked spreads iniquity.

20:15

There is gold, and an abundance of jewels;
But the lips of knowledge are a more precious
thing.

20:19

He who goes about as a slanderer reveals secrets,
Therefore do not associate with a gossip.

21:23

He who guards his mouth and his tongue,
Guards his soul from troubles.

22:11,12

He who loves purity of heart
And whose speech is gracious, the king is his friend.
[12]The eyes of the LORD preserve knowledge,
But He overthrows the words of the treacherous
man.

22:17,18

Incline your ear and hear the words of the wise,
And apply your mind to my knowledge;
[18]For it will be pleasant if you keep them within you,
That they may be ready on your lips.

23:15,16

My son, if your heart is wise,
My own heart also will be glad;
[16]And my inmost being will rejoice,
When your lips speak what is right.

24:1,2

Do not be envious of evil men,
Nor desire to be with them;
[2]For their minds devise violence,
And their lips talk of trouble.

24:26

He kisses the lips
Who gives a right answer.

24:28

Do not be a witness against your neighbor without
cause,
And do not deceive with your lips.

25:8-15

Do not go out hastily to argue your case:
Otherwise, what will you do in the end,
When your neighbor puts you to shame?
^{9}Argue your case with your neighbor,
And do not reveal the secret of another.
^{10}Lest he who hears it reproach you,
And the evil report about you not pass away.
^{11}Like apples of gold in settings of silver
Is a word spoken in right circumstances.
^{12}Like an earring of gold and an ornament of fine
gold
Is a wise reprover to a listening ear.
^{13}Like the cold of snow in the time of harvest
Is a faithful messenger to those who send him,
For he refreshes the soul of his masters.
^{14}Like clouds and wind without rain
Is a man who boasts of his gifts falsely.
^{15}By forbearance a ruler may be persuaded,
And a soft tongue breaks the bone.

25:23

The north wind brings forth rain,
And a backbiting tongue, an angry countenance.

26:4,5

Do not answer a fool according to his folly,

Lest you also be like him.
⁵Answer a fool as his folly deserves,
Lest he be wise in his own eyes.

26:17-28

Like one who takes a dog by the ears
Is he who passes by and meddles with strife not
belonging to him.
¹⁸Like a madman who throws
Firebrands, arrows and death,
¹⁹So is the man who deceives his neighbor,
And says, "Was I not joking?"
²⁰For lack of wood the fire goes out,
And where there is no whisperer, contention quiets
down.
²¹Like charcoal to hot embers and wood to fire,
So is a contentious man to kindle strife.
²²The words of a whisperer are like dainty morsels,
And they go down into the innermost parts of the
body.
²³Like an earthen vessel overlaid with silver dross
Are burning lips and a wicked heart.
²⁴He who hates disguises it with his lips,
But he lays up deceit in his heart.
²⁵When he speaks graciously, do not believe
him,
For there are seven abominations in his heart.
²⁶Though his hatred covers itself with guile,
His wickedness will be revealed before the
assembly.
²⁷He who digs a pit will fall into it,
And he who rolls a stone, it will come back on him.
²⁸A lying tongue hates those it crushes,
And a flattering mouth works ruin.

27:2

Let another praise you, and not your own mouth;
A stranger, and not your own lips.

28:23

He who rebukes a man will afterward find more
favor
Than he who flatters with the tongue.

29:5

A man who flatters his neighbor
Is spreading a net for his steps.

29:20

Do you see a man who is hasty in his words?
There is more hope for a fool than for him.

30:10

Do not slander a slave to his master,
Lest he curse you and you be found guilty.

31:26 (Of the excellent wife)
She opens her mouth in wisdom,
And the teaching of kindness is on her tongue.

SURETYSHIP

6:1-5

My son, if you have become surety for your
neighbor,
Have given a pledge for a stranger,
[2]If you have been snared with the words of your
mouth,
Have been caught with the words of your mouth,
[3]Do this then, my son, and deliver yourself;
Since you have come into the hand of your
neighbor,
Go, humble yourself, and importune your
neighbor.
[4]Do not give sleep to your eyes,
Nor slumber to your eyelids;
[5]Deliver yourself like a gazelle from the hunter's
hand,
And like a bird from the hand of the fowler.

11:15

He who is surety for a stranger will surely suffer
for it,
But he who hates going surety is safe.

17:18

A man lacking in sense pledges,
And becomes surety in the presence of his
neighbor.

20:16

Take his garment when he becomes surety for a
stranger;

And for foreigners, hold him in pledge.

22:26,27

Do not be among those who give pledges,

Among those who become sureties for debts.

²⁷If you have nothing with which to pay,

Why should he take your bed from under you?

27:12,13

A prudent man sees evil and hides himself,

The naive proceed and pay the penalty.

¹³Take his garment when he becomes surety for a
stranger;

And for an adulteress woman hold him in pledge.

TRUTH

3:3,4

Do not let kindness and truth leave you;
Bind them around your neck,
Write them on the tablet of your heart.
[4]So you will find favor and good repute
In the sight of God and man.

8:6,7 (Wisdom speaking)

"Listen, for I shall speak noble things;
And the opening of my lips will produce right
things.
[7]For my mouth will utter truth;
And wickedness is an abomination to my lips."

12:17

He who speaks truth tells what is right,
But a false witness, deceit.

12:19

Truthful lips will be established forever,
But a lying tongue is only for a moment.

14:22

Will they not go astray who devise evil?
But kindness and truth will be to those who devise
good.

14:25

A truthful witness saves lives,
But he who speaks lies is treacherous.

143

16:6

> By lovingkindness and truth iniquity is atoned for,
> And by the fear of the LORD one keeps away from
> evil.

20:28

> Loyalty and truth preserve the king,
> And he upholds his throne by righteousness.

22:20,21

> Have I not written to you excellent things
> Of counsels and knowledge,
> ²¹To make you know the certainty of the words of
> truth
> That you may correctly answer to him who sent
> you?

23:23

> Buy truth, and do not sell it,
> Get wisdom and instruction and understanding.

29:14

> If a king judges the poor with truth,
> His throne will be established forever.

UNDERSTANDING*

(See also "Use of the Proverbs," "Wisdom")

2:1-6

>   My son, if you will receive my sayings,
>   And treasure my commandments within you,
>   ²Make your ear attentive to wisdom,
>   Incline your heart to understanding;
>   ³For if you cry for discernment,
>   Lift your voice for understanding;
>   ⁴If you seek her as silver,
>   And search for her as for hidden treasures;
>   ⁵Then you will discern the fear of the Lord,
>   And discover the knowledge of God.
>   ⁶For the Lord gives wisdom;
>   From His mouth come knowledge and
>   understanding.

2:11

>   Discretion will guard you,
>   Understanding will watch over you.

3:5

>   Trust in the Lord with all your heart,
>   And do not lean on your own understanding.

3:13

>   How blessed is the man who finds wisdom,
>   And the man who gains understanding.

*This English word translates four different Hebrew words.

3:19

The LORD by wisdom founded the earth;
By understanding He established the heavens.

4:1

Hear, O sons, the instruction of a father,
And give attention that you may gain
understanding.

4:5-7 (A father's words)

"Acquire wisdom! Acquire understanding!
Do not forget, nor turn away from the words of
my mouth.
⁶"Do not forsake her, and she will guard
you;
Love her, and she will watch over you.
⁷"The beginning of wisdom is: Acquire wisdom;
And with all your acquiring, get understanding."

5:1

My son, give attention to my wisdom,
Incline your ear to my understanding.

7:4

Say to wisdom, "You are my sister,"
And call understanding your intimate friend.

8:1

Does not wisdom call,
And understanding lift up her voice?

8:14 (Wisdom speaking)

"Counsel is mine and sound wisdom;
I am understanding, power is mine."

9:6 (Wisdom speaking)

"Forsake your folly and live,
And proceed in the way of understanding."

9:10

The fear of the LORD is the beginning of
wisdom,

And the knowledge of the Holy One is
    understanding.

10:13

On the lips of the discerning, wisdom is found,
But a rod is for the back of him who lacks
    understanding.

10:23

Doing wickedness is like sport to a fool;
And so is wisdom to a man of understanding.

11:12

He who despises his neighbor lacks sense,
But a man of understanding keeps silent.

13:15

Good understanding produces favor,
But the way of the treacherous is hard.

14:6

A scoffer seeks wisdom, and finds none,
But knowledge is easy to him who has
    understanding.

14:29

He who is slow to anger has great
    understanding,
But he who is quick-tempered exalts folly.

14:33

Wisdom rests in the heart of one who has
    understanding,
But in the bosom of fools it is made known.

15:21

Folly is joy to him who lacks sense,
But a man of understanding walks straight.

16:16

How much better it is to get wisdom than gold!

And to get understanding is to be chosen above
    silver.

16:22

Understanding is a fountain of life to him who
    has it,
But the discipline of fools is folly.

17:27

He who restrains his words has knowledge,
And he who has a cool spirit is a man of
    understanding.

18:2

A fool does not delight in understanding,
But only in revealing his own mind.

19:8

He who gets wisdom loves his own soul;
He who keeps understanding will find good.

19:25

Strike a scoffer and the naive may become
    shrewd,
But reprove one who has understanding and he
    will gain knowledge.

20:5

A plan in the heart of a man is like deep water,
But a man of understanding draws it out.

21:16

A man who wanders from the way of
    understanding
Will rest in the assembly of the dead.

21:30

There is no wisdom and no understanding
And no counsel against the Lord.

23:23

Buy truth, and do not sell it,
Get wisdom and instruction and understanding.

24:3

By wisdom a house is built,
And by understanding it is established.

28:16

A leader who is a great oppressor lacks
understanding,
But he who hates unjust gain will prolong his days.

USE OF THE PROVERBS

1:1-6

The proverbs of Solomon the son of David, king of
Israel:
[2]To know wisdom and instruction,
To discern the sayings of understanding,
[3]To receive instruction in wise behavior,
Righteousness, justice, and equity;
[4]To give prudence to the naive,
To the youth knowledge and discretion,
[5]A wise man will hear and increase in learning,
And a man of understanding will acquire wise
counsel,
[6]To understand a proverb and a figure,
The words of the wise and their riddles.

VIOLENCE

1:10-19

My son, if sinners entice you,
Do not consent.
[11]If they say, "Come with us,
Let us lie in wait for blood,
Let us ambush the innocent without cause;
[12]Let us swallow them alive like Sheol,
Even whole, as those who go down to the pit;
[13]We shall find all kinds of precious wealth,
We shall fill our houses with spoil;
[14]Throw in your lot with us,
We shall all have one purse."
[15]My son, do not walk in the way with them.
Keep your feet from their path,
[16]For their feet run to evil,
And they hasten to shed blood.
[17]Indeed, it is useless to spread the net
In the eyes of any bird;
[18]But they lie in wait for their own blood;
They ambush their own lives.
[19]So are the ways of everyone who gains by
violence;
It takes away the life of its possessors.

3:30-32

Do not contend with a man without cause,
If he has done you no harm.

³¹ Do not envy a man of violence,
And do not choose any of his ways.
³² For the crooked man is an abomination to
the LORD;
But He is intimate with the upright.

4:14-17

Do not enter the path of the wicked,
And do not proceed in the way of evil men.
¹⁵ Avoid it, do not pass by it;
Turn away from it and pass on.
¹⁶ For they cannot sleep unless they do evil;
And they are robbed of sleep unless they make
someone stumble.
¹⁷ For they eat the bread of wickedness,
And drink the wine of violence.

10:6

Blessings are on the head of the righteous,
But the mouth of the wicked conceals violence.

13:2

From the fruit of a man's mouth he enjoys good,
But the desire of the treacherous is violence.

16:29

A man of violence entices his neighbor,
And leads him in a way that is not good.

21:7

The violence of the wicked will drag them away,
Because they refuse to act with justice.

24:1,2

Do not be envious of evil men,
Nor desire to be with them;
² For their minds devise violence,
And their lips talk of trouble.

26:6
>He cuts off his own feet, and drinks violence
>Who sends a message by the hand of a fool.

29:10
>Men of bloodshed hate the blameless,
>But the upright are concerned for his life.

30:14
>There is a kind of man whose teeth are like swords,
>And his jaw teeth like knives,
>To devour the afflicted from the earth,
>And the needy from among men.

WEALTH

3:9,10

Honor the Lord from your wealth,
And from the first of all your produce;
¹⁰So your barns will be filled with plenty,
And your vats will overflow with new wine.

3:13-16

How blessed is the man who finds wisdom,
And the man who gains understanding.
¹⁴For its profit is better than the profit of
silver,
And its gain than fine gold.
¹⁵She is more precious than jewels;
And nothing you desire compares with her.
¹⁶Long life is in her right hand;
In her left hand are riches and honor.

8:10,11 (Wisdom speaking)

"Take my instruction, and not silver,
And knowledge rather than choicest gold.
¹¹"For wisdom is better than jewels;
And all desirable things can not compare with her."

8:18-21 (Wisdom speaking)

"Riches and honor are with me,
Enduring wealth and righteousness.
¹⁹"My fruit is better than gold, even pure gold,
And my yield than choicest silver.
²⁰"I walk in the way of righteousness,
In the midst of the paths of justice,

154

^{21}To endow those who love me with wealth,
That I may fill their treasuries."

10:2

Ill-gotten gains do not profit,
But righteousness delivers from death.

10:4

Poor is he who works with a negligent hand,
But the hand of the diligent makes rich.

10:15,16

The rich man's wealth is his fortress,
The ruin of the poor is their poverty.
^{16}The wages of the righteous is life,
The income of the wicked, punishment.

10:22

It is the blessing of the LORD that makes rich,
And He adds no sorrow to it.

11:4

Riches do not profit in the day of wrath,
But righteousness delivers from death.

11:16

A gracious woman attains honor,
And violent men attain riches.

11:28

He who trusts in his riches will fall,
But the righteous will flourish like the green leaf.

13:7,8

There is one who pretends to be rich, but has
nothing;
Another pretends to be poor, but has great wealth.
^{8}The ransom of a man's life is his riches,
But the poor hears no rebuke.

13:11

Wealth obtained by fraud dwindles,
But the one who gathers by labor increases it.

13:21,22

Adversity pursues sinners,
But the righteous will be rewarded with prosperity.
²³A good man leaves an inheritance to his children's
children,
And the wealth of the sinner is stored up for the
righteous.

14:4

Where no oxen are, the manger is clean,
But much increase comes by the strength of the ox.

14:20

The poor is hated even by his neighbor,
But those who love the rich are many.

14:23,24

In all labor there is profit,
But mere talk leads only to poverty.
²⁴The crown of the wise is their riches,
But the folly of fools is foolishness.

15:6

Much wealth is in the house of the righteous,
But trouble is in the income of the wicked.

15:16,17

Better is a little with the fear of the LORD,
Than great treasure and turmoil with it.
¹⁷Better is a dish of vegetables where love is,
Than a fattened ox and hatred with it.

15:27

He who profits illicitly troubles his own
house,

But he who hates bribes will live.

16:8

Better is a little with righteousness
Than great income with injustice.

16:16

How much better it is to get wisdom than gold!
And to get understanding is to be chosen above
    silver.

17:8

A bribe is a charm in the sight of its owner;
Wherever he turns, he prospers.

18:11

A rich man's wealth is his strong city,
And like a high wall in his own imagination.

19:4

Wealth adds many friends,
But a poor man is separated from his friend.

19:10

Luxury is not fitting for a fool;
Much less for a slave to rule over princes.

19:14

House and wealth are an inheritance from fathers,
But a prudent wife is from the LORD.

20:14

"Bad, bad," says the buyer;
But when he goes his way, then he boasts.

20:21

An inheritance gained hurriedly at the beginning,
Will not be blessed in the end.

21:6

The getting of treasures by a lying tongue

Is a fleeting vapor, the pursuit of death.

21:17

He who loves pleasure will become a poor man;
He who loves wine and oil will not become rich.

21:20

There is precious treasure and oil in the dwelling of
the wise,
But a foolish man swallows it up.

22:1

A good name is to be more desired than great
riches,
Favor is better than silver and gold.

22:4

The reward of humility and the fear of the LORD
Are riches, honor and life.

22:16

He who oppresses the poor to make much for
himself
Or who gives to the rich, will only come to poverty.

23:4,5

Do not weary yourself to gain wealth,
Cease from your consideration of it.
⁵When you set your eyes on it, it is gone.
For wealth certainly makes itself wings,
Like an eagle that flies toward the heavens.

24:3,4

By wisdom a house is built,
And by understanding it is established;
⁴And by knowledge the rooms are filled
With all precious and pleasant riches.

27:23,24

Know well the condition of your flocks,

And pay attention to your herds;
²⁴For riches are not forever,
Nor does a crown endure to all generations.

28:8

He who increases his wealth by interest and usury,
Gathers it for him who is gracious to the poor.

28:19,20

He who tills his land will have plenty of food,
But he who follows empty pursuits will have
poverty in plenty.
²⁰A faithful man will abound with blessings,
But he who makes haste to be rich will not go
unpunished.

28:22

A man with an evil eye hastens after wealth,
And does not know that want will come upon him.

28:25

An arrogant man stirs up strife,
But he who trusts in the LORD will prosper.

30:7-9

Two things I asked of Thee,
Do not refuse me before I die:
⁸Keep deception and lies far from me,
Give me neither poverty nor riches;
Feed me with the food that is my portion,
⁹Lest I be full and deny Thee and say,
"Who is the LORD?"
Or lest I be in want and steal,
And profane the name of my God.

THE WICKED

A. General

3:25,26

    Do not be afraid of sudden fear,

    Nor of the onslaught of the wicked when it comes;

    [26]For the LORD will be your confidence,

    And will keep your foot from being caught.

4:14-19

    Do not enter the path of the wicked,

    And do not proceed in the way of evil men.

    [15]Avoid it, do not pass by it;

    Turn away from it and pass on.

    [16]For they cannot sleep unless they do evil;

    And they are robbed of sleep unless they make
        someone stumble.

    [17]For they eat the bread of wickedness,

    And drink the wine of violence.

    [18]But the path of the righteous is like the light
        of dawn,

    That shines brighter and brighter until the full day.

    [19]The way of the wicked is like darkness;

    They do not know over what they stumble.

5:22,23

    His own iniquities will capture the wicked,

    And he will be held with the cords of his sin.

    [23]He will die for lack of instruction,

    And in the greatness of his folly he will go astray.

6:12-15

A worthless person, a wicked man,
Is the one who walks with a false mouth,
^{13}Who winks with his eyes, who signals with his feet,
Who points with his fingers;
^{14}Who with perversity in his heart devises evil
continually,
Who spreads strife.
^{15}Therefore his calamity will come suddenly;
Instantly he will be broken, and there will be no
healing.

8:7 (Wisdom speaking)

"For my mouth will utter truth;
And wickedness is an abomination to my lips."

9:7

He who corrects a scoffer gets dishonor for himself,
And he who reproves a wicked man gets insults for
himself.

10:27

The fear of the LORD prolongs life,
But the years of the wicked will be shortened.

13:17

A wicked messenger falls into adversity,
But a faithful envoy brings healing.

16:4

The LORD has made everything for its own
purpose,
Even the wicked for the day of evil.

16:12

It is an abomination for kings to commit
wickedness,
For a throne is established on righteousness.

17:4

An evildoer listens to wicked lips.
A liar pays attention to a destructive tongue.

17:15

He who justifies the wicked, and he who condemns
the righteous.
Both of them alike are an abomination to the Lord.

17:19

He who loves transgression loves strife:
He who raises his door seeks destruction.

17:23

A wicked man receives a bribe from the bosom
To pervert the ways of justice.

18:3

When a wicked man comes, contempt also comes,
And with dishonor comes reproach.

19:28

A rascally witness makes a mockery of justice,
And the mouth of the wicked spreads iniquity.

20:26

A wise king winnows the wicked,
And drives the threshing wheel over them.

21:4

Haughty eyes and a proud heart,
The lamp of the wicked, is sin.

21:7

The violence of the wicked will drag them away,
Because they refuse to act with justice.

21:10

The soul of the wicked desires evil:
His neighbor finds no favor in his eyes.

21:27

The sacrifice of the wicked is an abomination.
How much more when he brings it with evil intent!

22:8

He who sows iniquity will reap vanity.
And the rod of his fury will perish.

24:19,20

Do not fret yourself because of evildoers.
Or be envious of the wicked;
^{20}For there will be no future for the evil man;
The lamp of the wicked will be put out.

24:24,25

He who says to the wicked, "You are righteous,"
Peoples will curse him, nations will abhor him;
^{25}But to those who rebuke the wicked will be delight.
And a good blessing will come upon them.

25:5

Take away the wicked from before the king.
And his throne will be established in righteousness.

26:23-26

Like an earthen vessel overlaid with silver dross
Are burning lips and a wicked heart.
^{24}He who hates disguises it with his lips,
But he lays up deceit in his heart.
^{25}When he speaks graciously, do not believe him,
For there are seven abominations in his heart.
^{26}Though his hatred covers itself with guile,
His wickedness will be revealed before the assembly.

28:4

Those who forsake the law praise the wicked.
But those who keep the law strive with them.

28:15

> Like a roaring lion and a rushing bear
> Is a wicked ruler over a poor people.

29:12

> If a ruler pays attention to falsehood,
> All his ministers become wicked.

29:24

> He who is a partner with a thief hates his own life:
> He hears the oath but tells nothing.

B. *The Wicked Contrasted With the Righteous:* (See
   "The Righteous")

WISDOM

(See also "Use of the Proverbs")

1:7

The fear of the Lord is the beginning of knowledge;
Fools despise wisdom and instruction.

1:20-33

Wisdom shouts in the street,
She lifts her voice in the square;
^{21}At the head of the noisy streets she cries out;
At the entrance of the gates in the city, she utters
her sayings:
^{22}"How long, O naive ones, will you love simplicity?
And scoffers delight themselves in scoffing,
And fools hate knowledge?
^{23}"Turn to my reproof,
Behold, I will pour out my spirit on you;
I will make my words known to you.
^{24}Because I called, and you refused;
I stretched out my hand, and no one paid attention;
^{25}And you neglected all my counsel,
And did not want my reproof;
^{26}I will even laugh at your calamity;
I will mock when your dread comes,
^{27}When your dread comes like a storm,
And your calamity comes on like a whirlwind,
When distress and anguish come on you.
^{28}"Then they will call on me, but I will not answer;
They will seek me diligently, but they shall not find
me,
^{29}Because they hated knowledge,
And did not choose the fear of the Lord.

³⁰"They would not accept my counsel,
They spurned all my reproof.
³¹"So they shall eat of the fruit of their own way,
And be satiated with their own devices.
³²"For the waywardness of the naive shall kill them,
And the complacency of fools shall destroy them.
³³"But he who listens to me shall live securely,
And shall be at ease from the dread of evil."

2:1-12

My son, if you will receive my sayings,
And treasure my commandments within you,
²Make your ear attentive to wisdom,
Incline your heart to understanding;
³For if you cry for discernment,
Lift your voice for understanding;
⁴If you seek her as silver,
And search for her as for hidden treasures;
⁵Then you will discern the fear of the LORD,
And discover the knowledge of God.
⁶For the LORD gives wisdom;
From His mouth come knowledge and
          understanding.
⁷He stores up sound wisdom for the upright;
He is a shield to those who walk in integrity,
⁸Guarding the paths of justice,
And He preserves the way of His godly ones.
⁹Then you will discern righteousness and justice
And equity and every good course.
¹⁰For wisdom will enter your heart,
And knowledge will be pleasant to your soul;
¹¹Discretion will guard you,
Understanding will watch over you,
¹²To deliver you from the way of evil. . . .

3:13-23

How blessed is the man who finds wisdom,
And the man who gains understanding.
[14]For its profit is better than the profit of silver,
And its gain than fine gold.
[15]She is more precious than jewels;
And nothing you desire compares with her.
[16]Long life is in her right hand;
In her left hand are riches and honor.
[17]Her ways are pleasant ways,
And all her paths are peace.
[18]She is a tree of life to those who take hold of her,
And happy are all who hold her fast.
[19]The LORD by wisdom founded the earth;
By understanding He established the heavens.
[20]By His knowledge the deeps were broken up,
And the skies drip with dew.
[21]My son, let them not depart from your sight;
Keep sound wisdom and discretion,
[22]So they will be life to your soul,
And adornment to your neck.
[23]Then you will walk in your way securely,
And your foot will not stumble.

4:3-9

When I was a son to my father,
Tender and the only son in the sight of my mother,
[4]Then he taught me and said to me,
"Let your heart hold fast my words;
Keep my commandments and live;
[5]Acquire wisdom! Acquire understanding!
Do not forget, nor turn away from the words of my
mouth.
[6]"Do not forsake her, and she will guard you;
Love her, and she will watch over you.

[7]"The beginning of wisdom is: Acquire wisdom;
And with all your acquiring, get understanding.
[8]"Prize her, and she will exalt you;
She will honor you if you embrace her.
[9]"She will place on your head a garland of grace;
She will present you with a crown of beauty."

4:10-12

Hear, my son, and accept my sayings,
And the years of your life will be many.
[11]"I have directed you in the way of wisdom;
I have led you in upright paths.
[12]When you walk, your steps will not be impeded;
And if you run, you will not stumble.

5:1,2

My son, give attention to my wisdom,
Incline your ear to my understanding;
[2]That you may observe discretion,
And your lips may reserve knowledge.

7:4,5

Say to wisdom, "You are my sister,"
And call understanding your intimate friend;
[5]That they may keep you from an adulteress,
From the foreigner who flatters with her words.

8:1-36

Does not wisdom call,
And understanding lift up her voice?
[2]On top of the heights beside the way,
Where the paths meet, she takes her stand;
[3]Beside the gates, at the opening to the city,
At the entrance of the doors, she cries out:
[4]"To you, O men, I call,
And my voice is to the sons of men.

⁵"O naive ones, discern prudence;
  And, O fools, discern wisdom.
⁶"Listen, for I shall speak noble things;
  And the opening of my lips will produce right
      things.
⁷"For my mouth will utter truth;
  And wickedness is an abomination to my lips.
⁸"All the utterances of my mouth are in
      righteousness;
  There is nothing crooked or perverted in them.
⁹"They are all straightforward to him who
      understands,
  And right to those who find knowledge.
¹⁰"Take my instruction, and not silver,
  And knowledge rather than choicest gold.
¹¹"For wisdom is better than jewels;
  And all desirable things can not compare with her.

¹²"I, wisdom, dwell with pruduce,
  And I find knowledge and discretion.
¹³"The fear of the Lord is to hate evil;
  Pride and arrogance and the evil way,
  And the perverted mouth, I hate.
¹⁴"Counsel is mine and sound wisdom;
  I am understanding, power is mine.
¹⁵"By me kings reign,
  And rulers decree justice.
¹⁶"By me princes rule, and nobles,
  All who judge rightly.
¹⁷"I love those who love me;
  And those who diligently seek me will find me.
¹⁸"Riches and honor are with me,
  Enduring wealth and righteousness.
¹⁹"My fruit is better than gold, even pure gold,

And my yield than choicest silver.
²⁰"I walk in the way of righteousness.
In the midst of the paths of justice.
²¹To endow those who love me with wealth.
That I may fill their treasuries.

²²"The LORD possessed me at the beginning of His way.
Before His works of old.
²³"From everlasting I was established.
From the beginning, from the earliest times of the
earth.
²⁴"When there were no depths I was brought forth.
When there were no springs abounding with water.
²⁵"Before the mountains were settled.
Before the hills I was brought forth.
²⁶While He had not yet made the earth and the fields.
Nor the first dust of the world.
²⁷"When He established the heavens. I was there.
When He inscribed a circle on the face of the deep.
²⁸When He made firm the skies above.
When the springs of the deep became fixed.
²⁹When He set for the sea its boundary.
So that the water should not transgress His
command.
When He marked out the foundations of the earth:
³⁰Then I was beside Him. as a master workman;
And I was daily His delight.
Rejoicing always before Him.
³¹Rejoicing in the world. His earth.
And having my delight in the sons of men.

³²"Now therefore. O sons. listen to me.
For blessed are they who keep my ways.
³³"Heed instruction and be wise.

And do not neglect it.
³⁴"Blessed is the man who listens to me,
Watching daily at my gates,
Waiting at my doorposts.
³⁵"For he who finds me finds life,
And obtains favor from the LORD.
³⁶"But he who sins against me injures himself;
All those who hate me love death."

9:1-6

Wisdom has built her house,
She has hewn out her seven pillars;
²She has prepared her food, she has mixed her
wine;
She has also set her table;
³She has sent out her maidens, she calls
From the tops of the heights of the city:
⁴"Whoever is naive, let him turn in here!"
To him who lacks understanding she says,
⁵"Come, eat of my food,
And drink of the wine I have mixed.
⁶"Forsake your folly and live,
And proceed in the way of understanding."

9:10-12

The fear of the LORD is the beginning of wisdom,
And the knowledge of the Holy One is understanding.
¹¹For by me your days will be multiplied,
And years of life will be added to you.
¹²If you are wise, you are wise for yourself,
And if you scoff, you alone will bear it.

10:13

On the lips of the discerning, wisdom is found,
But a rod is for the back of him who lacks
understanding.

10:23

Doing wickedness is like sport to a fool:
And so is wisdom to a man of understanding.

10:31

The mouth of the righteous flows with wisdom,
But the perverted tongue will be cut out.

11:2

When pride comes, then comes dishonor,
But with the humble is wisdom.

13:10

Through presumption comes nothing but strife,
But with those who receive counsel is wisdom.

14:6

A scoffer seeks wisdom, and finds none,
But knowledge is easy to him who has understanding.

14:8

The wisdom of the prudent is to understand his way,
But the folly of fools is deceit.

14:33

Wisdom rests in the heart of one who has
      understanding,
But in the bosom of fools it is made known.

15:33

The fear of the LORD is the instruction for wisdom,
And before honor comes humility.

16:16

How much better it is to get wisdom than gold!
And to get understanding is to be chosen above silver.

17:16

Why is there a price in the hand of a fool to buy
      wisdom,

When he has no sense?

17:24

Wisdom is in the presence of the one who has
 understanding.
But the eyes of a fool are on the ends of the
 earth.

18:1

He who separates himself seeks his own desire.
He quarrels against all sound wisdom.

18:4

The words of a man's mouth are deep waters:
The fountain of wisdom is a bubbling brook.

19:8

He who gets wisdom loves his own soul:
He who keeps understanding will find good.

20:12

The hearing ear and the seeing eye.
The LORD has made both of them.

21:30

There is no wisdom and no understanding
And no counsel against the LORD.

23:9

Do not speak in the hearing of a fool.
For he will despise the wisdom of your words.

23:23

Buy truth, and do not sell it,
Get wisdom and instruction and understanding.

24:3

By wisdom a house is built,
And by understanding it is established.

24:7

Wisdom is too high for a fool,

He does not open his mouth in the gate.

24:13, 14
My son, eat honey, for it is good.
Yes, the honey from the comb is sweet to your taste:
[14]Know that wisdom is thus for your soul:
If you find it, then there will be a future,
And your hope will not be cut off.

29:3
A man who loves wisdom makes his father glad.
But he who keeps company with harlots wastes his
wealth.

29:15
The rod and reproof give wisdom,
But a child who gets his own way brings shame to his
mother.

31:26 (Of the excellent wife)
She opens her mouth in wisdom,
And the teaching of kindness is on her tongue.

THE WISE

A. General (See also "Use of the Proverbs")

3:7

Do not be wise in your own eyes:
Fear the LORD and turn away from evil.

9:8,9

Do not reprove a scoffer, lest he hate you,
Reprove a wise man, and he will love you.
⁹Give instructions to a wise man, and he will be
still wiser,
Teach a righteous man, and he will increase his
learning.

10:5

He who gathers in summer is a son who acts wisely,
But he who sleeps in harvest is a son who acts
shamefully.

10:19

When there are many words, transgression is
unavoidable,
But he who restrains his lips is wise.

11:29,30

He who troubles his own house will inherit wind,
And the foolish will be servant to the wisehearted.
³⁰The fruit of the righteous is a tree of life,
And he who is wise wins souls.

12:18

There is one who speaks rashly like the thrusts of a
    sword,
But the tongue of the wise brings healing.

13:1

A wise son accepts his father's discipline,
But a scoffer does not listen to rebuke.

13:14

The teaching of the wise is a fountain of life,
To turn aside from the snares of death.

14:35

The king's favor is toward a servant who acts wisely,
But his anger is toward him who acts shamefully.

15:12

A scoffer does not love one who reproves him,
He will not go to the wise.

15:24

The path of life leads upward for the wise,
That he may keep away from Sheol below.

15:31

He whose ear listens to the life-giving reproof
Will dwell among the wise.

16:14

The wrath of a king is as messengers of death,
But a wise man will appease it.

16:21

The wise in heart will be called discerning,
And sweetness of speech increases persuasiveness.

16:23

The heart of the wise teaches his mouth,
And adds persuasiveness to his lips.

17:2

> A servant who acts wisely will rule
>> over a son who acts shamefully,
> And will share in the inheritance among brothers.

18:15

> The mind of the prudent acquires knowledge,
> And the ear of the wise seeks knowledge.

19:14

> House and wealth are an inheritance from fathers,
> But a prudent wife is from the LORD.

20:26

> A wise king winnows the wicked,
> And drives the threshing wheel over them.

21:11

> When the scoffer is punished, the naive becomes
>> wise;
> But when the wise is instructed, he receives
>> knowledge.

21:22

> A wise man scales the city of the mighty,
> And brings down the stronghold in which they
>> trust.

22:17,18

> Incline your ear and hear the words of the wise,
> And apply your mind to my knowledge;
> [18]For it will be pleasant if you keep them
>> within you,
> That they may be ready on your lips.

23:24

> The father of the righteous will greatly rejoice,
> And he who begets a wise son will be glad in him.

24:5

> A wise man is strong,
> And a man of knowledge increases power.

25:12

> Like an earring of gold and an ornament of fine
>   gold
> Is a wise reprover to a listening ear.

26:12

> Do you see a man wise in his own eyes?
> There is more hope for a fool than for him.

29:8

> Scorners set a city aflame,
> But wise men turn away anger.

30:24-28

> Four things are small on the earth,
> But they are exceedingly wise:
> [25]The ants are not a strong folk,
> But they prepare their food in summer;
> [26]The badgers are not mighty folk,
> Yet they make their houses in the rocks;
> [27]The locusts have no king,
> Yet all of them go out in ranks;
> [28]The lizard you may grasp with the hands,
> Yet it is in kings' palaces.

B. The Wise Contrasted with the Fool (See "The Fool")

WOMAN

2:10,11,16,17

    For wisdom will enter your heart,
    And knowledge will be pleasant to your soul;
[11]Discretion will guard you,
    Understanding will watch over you . . .
[16]To deliver you from the strange woman,
    From the adulteress who flatters with her words;
[17]That leaves the companion of her youth,
    And forgets the covenant of her God.

5:15-20

    Drink water from your own cistern,
    And fresh water from your own well.
[16]Should your springs be dispersed abroad,
    Streams of water in the streets?
[17]Let them be yours alone,
    And not for strangers with you.
[18]Let your fountain be blessed,
    And rejoice in the wife of your youth.
[19]As a loving hind and a graceful doe,
    Let her breasts satisfy you at all times;
    Be exhilarated always with her love.
[20]For why should you, my son, be exhilarated with an
        adulteress,
    And embrace the bosom of a foreigner?

6:23-33

    For the commandment is a lamp, and the teaching
        is light;

And reproofs for discipline are the way of life,
²⁴To keep you from the evil woman,
From the smooth tongue of the adulteress.
²⁵Do not desire her beauty in your heart,
Nor let her catch you with her eyelids.
²⁶For on account of a harlot one is reduced to a loaf of
bread,
And an adulteress hunts for the precious life.
²⁷Can a man take fire in his bosom,
And his clothes not be burned?
²⁸Or can a man walk on hot coals,
And his feet not be scorched?
²⁹So is the one who goes in to his neighbor's
wife;
Whoever touches her will not go unpunished.
³⁰Men do not despise a thief if he steals
To satisfy himself when he is hungry;
³¹But when he is found, he must repay
sevenfold;
He must give all the substance of his house.
³²The one who commits adultery with a woman is
lacking sense;
He who would destroy himself does it.
³³Wounds and disgrace he will find,
And his reproach will not be blotted out.

7:4,5

Say to wisdom, "You are my sister,"
And call understanding your intimate friend;
⁵That they may keep you from an adulteress,
From the foreigner who flatters with her words.

9:13

The woman of folly is boisterous,
She is naive, and knows nothing.

11:16

> A gracious woman attains honor,
> And violent men attain riches.

11:22

> As a ring of gold in a swine's snout,
> So is a beautiful woman who lacks discretion.

12:4

> An excellent wife is the crown of her husband,
> But she who shames him is as rottenness in his
>   bones.

14:1

> The wise woman builds her house,
> But the foolish tears it down with her own hands.

18:22

> He who finds a wife finds a good thing,
> And obtains favor from the LORD.

19:13,14

> A foolish son is destruction to his father,
> And the contentions of a wife are a constant dripping.
> [14]House and wealth are an inheritance from fathers,
> But a prudent wife is from the LORD.

21:9

> It is better to live in a corner of a roof,
> Than in a house shared with a contentious woman.

21:19

> It is better to live in a desert land,
> Than with a contentious and vexing woman.

25:24

> It is better to live in a corner of the roof
> Than in a house shared with a contentious woman.

27:15,16

> A constant dripping on a day of steady rain

And a contentious woman are alike;
[16]He who would restrain her restrains the wind,
And grasps oil with his right hand.

30:20

This is the way of an adulteress woman:
She eats and wipes her mouth,
And says, "I have done no wrong."

31:10-31

An excellent wife, who can find?
For her worth is far above jewels.
[11]The heart of her husband trusts in her,
And he will have no lack of gain.
[12]She does him good and not evil
All the days of her life.
[13]She looks for wool and flax,
And works with her hands in delight.
[14]She is like merchant ships:
She brings her food from afar.
[15]She rises also while it is still night,
And gives food to her household,
And portions to her maidens.
[16]She considers a field and buys it;
From her earnings she plants a vineyard.
[17]She girds herself with strength,
And makes her arms strong.
[18]She senses that her gain is good;
Her lamp does not go out at night.
[19]She stretches out her hands to the distaff,
And her hands grasp the spindle.
[20]She extends her hand to the poor;
And she stretches out her hands to the needy.
[21]She is not afraid of the snow for her household,
For all her household are clothed with scarlet.

²²She makes coverings for herself:
Her clothing is fine linen and purple.
²³Her husband is known in the gates,
When he sits among the elders of the land.
²⁴She makes linen garments and sells them,
And supplies belts to the tradesmen.
²⁵Strength and dignity are her clothing,
And she smiles at the future.
²⁶She opens her mouth in wisdom,
And the teaching of kindness is on her tongue.
²⁷She looks well to the ways of her household,
And does not eat the bread of idleness.
²⁸Her children rise up and bless her;
Her husband also, and he praises her, saying:
²⁹"Many daughters have done nobly,
But you excel them all."
³⁰Charm is deceitful and beauty is vain,
But a woman who fears the LORD, she shall be
    praised.
³¹Give her the product of her hands,
And let her works praise her in the gates.

THE WORD OF GOD

2:6

> . . . the LORD gives wisdom;
> From His mouth come knowledge and
>   understanding.

13:13

> The one who despises the word will be in debt to
>   it,
> But the one who fears the commandment will be
>   rewarded.

16:20

> He who gives attention to the word shall find
>   good,
> And blessed is he who trusts in the LORD.

29:18

> Where there is no vision [revelation], the people
>   are unrestrained,
> But happy is he who keeps the law.

30:5,6

> Every word of God is tested;
> He is a shield to those who take refuge in Him.
> [6]Do not add to His words
> Lest he reprove you, and you be proved a liar.

WORK

10:4

      Poor is he who works with a negligent
          hand,
      But the hand of the diligent makes rich.

12:11,12

      He who tills his land will have plenty of bread,
      But he who pursues vain things lacks sense.
    ¹²The wicked desires the booty of evil men,
      But the root of the righteous yields fruit.

14:23

      In all labor there is profit,
      But mere talk leads only to poverty.

16:26

      A worker's appetite works for him,
      For his hunger urges him on.

18:9

      He also who is slack in his work
      Is brother to him who destroys.

22:29

      Do you see a man skilled in his work?
      He will stand before kings;
      He will not stand before obscure men.

24:27

      Prepare your work outside,
      And make it ready for yourself in the field;
      Afterwards, then, build your house.

27:18

      He who tends the fig tree will eat its fruit;
      And he who cares for his master will be honored.

28:19

> He who tills his land will have plenty of food,
> But he who follows empty pursuits will have
> poverty in plenty.

31:13-31 (About the excellent wife)

> She looks for wool and flax,
> And works with her hands in delight.
> [14]She is like merchant ships;
> She brings her food from afar.
> [15]She rises also while it is still night,
> And gives food to her household.
> And portions to her maidens.
> [16]She considers a field and buys it;
> From her earnings she plants a vineyard.
> [17]She girds herself with strength,
> And makes her arms strong.
> [18]She senses that her gain is good:
> Her lamp does not go out at night.
> [19]She stretches out her hands to the distaff,
> And her hands grasp the spindle.
> [20]She extends her hand to the poor;
> And she stretches out her hands to the needy.
> [21]She is not afraid of the snow for her household,
> For all her household are clothed with scarlet.
> [22]She makes coverings for herself;
> Her clothing is fine linen and purple.
> [23]Her husband is known in the gates,
> When he sits among the elders of the land.
> [24]She makes linen garments and sells them,
> And supplies belts to the tradesmen.   . .
> [27]She looks well to the ways of her household,
> And does not eat the bread of idleness. . . . .
> [31]Give her the product of her hands,
> And let her works praise her in the gates.